Run to Win

The Training Secrets of the Kenyan Runners

Jürg Wirz

Run to Win

The Training Secrets of the Kenyan Runners

MEYER
& MEYER
SPORT

British Library Cataloguing in Publication Data
A catalogue record for this book is available from the British Library

Jürg Wirz
Run to Win
The Training Secrets of the Kenyan Runners
Oxford: Meyer & Meyer Sport (UK) Ltd., 2006
ISBN 10: 1-84126-188-2
ISBN 13: 978-1-84126-188-1

© 2006 by Meyer & Meyer Sport (UK) Ltd.
Aachen, Adelaide, Auckland, Budapest, Graz, Johannesburg,
New York, Olten (CH), Oxford, Singapore, Toronto
Member of the World
Sports Publishers' Association (WSPA)
www.w-s-p-a.org
Printed and bound by: B.O.S.S Druck und Medien GmbH, Germany
ISBN 10: 1-84126-188-2
ISBN 13: 978-1-84126-188-1
E-Mail: verlag@m-m-sports.com
www.m-m-sports.com

CONTENTS

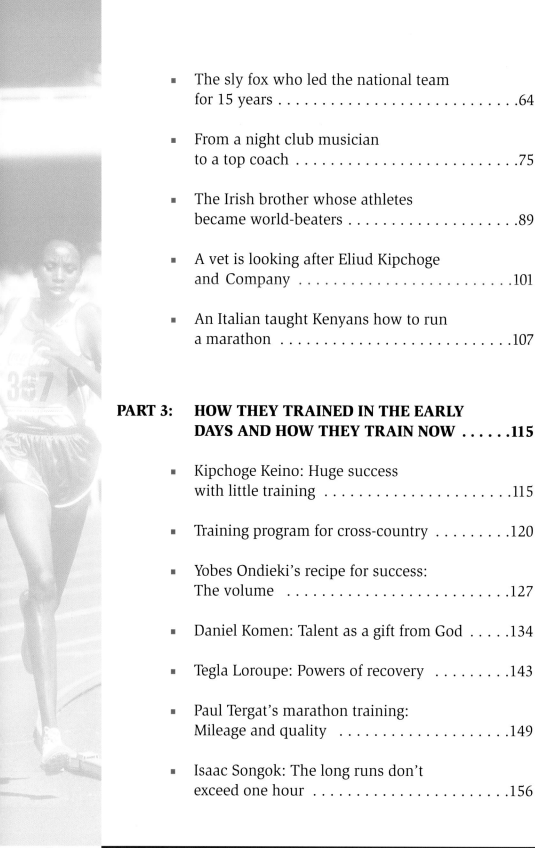

INTRODUCTION

It all began with Abebe Bikila. Ancient Rome lent character to the Olympic Games of 1960. It was a ghostly scene on the evening of September 10, the evening of the marathon. Rome's historic monuments shone in the full brightness of the floodlights and contrasted heavily with the night. In the pale headlights of the cars that followed the runners through the Eternal City, Abebe Bikila ran towards the finish line, barefoot and not pressed at all by the Moroccan Rhadi Ben Abdesselem, who came in second place. When the lean soldier of Haile Selassie's bodyguard ended the 42.195 kilometers as the first African Olympic Champion, it wasn't only the Romans who were ecstatic.

Back in 1928, the Algerian, Boughera El Quafi, had already won an Olympic marathon as a team member of France, but Abebe Bikila's victory formed the prelude to the East African advance in the world of athletics. It was the beginning of a superiority that, particularly in the past 20 years, has become more and more intense. Until then, the Europeans had dominated the running scene, from time to time interrupted by the USA, New Zealand or Australia.

Five years after the foundation of the Kenyan National Athletics Federation, K.A.A.A., in 1951, Ethiopia's neighbor in to south participated for the first time at the Olympic Games. Twelve years later, in Mexico City, Kenya celebrated its first Olympic Champion when Naftali Temu won the 10,000 meters. In the same year, 1968, Kipchoge Keino, today the chairman of the National Olympic Committee, won his first of two gold medals.

The boycotts of 1976 and 1980 were a major setback for Kenyan sports. But not for long. Today Kipchoge Keino's country is dominating all the running events for men from 800 meters to marathon. In the year 2005 in the half-marathon, there were 66 Kenyans among the first 100 in the world, but only ten Ethiopians!

In this book, we show how Kenya became the world's No. 1 running nation within a generation. You will get to know the people who took part in waking up this sleeping giant and the ones who are still involved. You will become acquainted with the training philosophies and training programs of the former and current stars. Kip Keino, who was at the top almost 40 years ago, had to rely on his memories, because nobody kept a diary at the time he was a champion. But when we talk about such runners as Yobes Ondieki, Daniel Komen, Tegla Loroupe, Paul Tergat or Saif Saaeed Shaheen, a.k.a. Stephen Cherono, all the programs are taken from the authentic transcripts of their training diaries.

We explore the socio-cultural backgrounds of the Kenyan marvels, as well as the newest scientific findings about genetic advantages over the European and the American athletes. I have been privileged to live in Kenya since 1999 as a journalist and a writer, more precisely in Eldoret, the town where more athletic greats live than anywhere else in the world. Kipchoge Keino, Yobes Ondieki, Patrick Sang, Ibrahim Hussein, Noah Ngeny, Daniel Komen, Moses Kiptanui, Moses Tanui, Bernard Barmasai, Benjamin Limo, Eliud Kipchoge, Saif Saaeed Shaheen and Sammy Korir are some of them.

A landscape made for running

Kenya is a very fascinating part of the world with an absolutely beautiful landscape, that is full of contrasts. You may only be able to understand this country if you are ready to accept it the way it is, with all its inconsistencies. Average Kenyans are friendly people but not always honest. For a "muzungu," a white person, it is sometimes difficult to understand their thoughts. Indeed, as long as people look at the Kenyans with a European mentality, they will always remain strangers.

Kenya is a different world. Like most other Africans, Kenyans live for the "here and now" and don't think too much about the future. Thus, it might happen that somebody starts constructing a house but after building the foundation walls

He has to stop because he is running out of money. Kenyan women are far from having equal rights. They are meant to do the hard work at home. Kids learn how to write and read when they are three or four years old, and in school there are high standards of discipline; they get an education as though they were going to earn a living in London one day. There they studied where the Thames and Rhine run instead of being prepared for a life in difficult surroundings.

Women are the heavy laborers

Even the many missionaries and Western church representatives making their living in Kenya seem to be more intent in getting new members for their churches than offering the most important help for self-preservation. Frankly, I prefer the "missionaries" who have come to Kenya in the past 20 years to teach young, hungry runners the right training methods and helped them to get a new, better life.

I wish to express my gratitude to all the persons who made this book possible. At the same time, I apologize to our female readers for the fact that the vast majority of the people mentioned in the book are men. There is a simple reason for that: There were no women playing a decisive role in the development of athletics in Kenya and even in the 21st century most of the world-class athletes coming from Kenya are male.

For the title of the book, we decided to choose "Run to Win" because it applies perfectly to the mentality of the Kenyan athletes.

Eldoret/Kenya, Spring 2006

Jürg Wirz

PART 1: FACTS AND FIGURES

ON THE DOUBLE THROUGH HISTORY

In the early days of mankind, those who best adapted survived ecological changes and later learned how to make use of primitive tools and snatch something away from the wild animals' hunt. Only the cleverest of our ancestors survived and passed their genetic make-up to the next generation.

According to today's knowledge, it was not only *Homo erectus* who lived 1.6 million years ago, that has his origin in East Africa but also *Homo sapiens*. From there, 40,000 to 50,000 years ago he moved in the footsteps of his archaic forefathers to Asia and Europe and drove away the early human beings. The huge Rift Valley, which is almost 6,000 kilometers long, and stretches from the Jordan Valley through the Red Sea, Ethiopia, Kenya and Tanzania southward through Africa, developed 20 million years ago and cuts Kenya in two. The Rift Valley is believed to be the birth place of mankind. But this former Garden of Eden also has its perils: Drought, population explosion, deadly diseases and economic chaos are constant threats. Kenya is fighting for its future.

The wealth of the small elite is vast in contrast to the impoverishment of the large majority. Fifty percent of the population has to manage with less than $ 1 US a day. At the beginning of 2003, at one of their first sittings under the Kibaki government, members of parliament raised their basic salaries to 500,000 Ksh (approximately $ 6,500 US) a month, allowances not included. This is almost half of the salary a U.S. representative is earning. In Kenya, a member of parliament earns 160 times more than the average citizen.

Nairobi at the beginning of the 20th century

Against this background, it is understandable that many young Kenyans have only one dream: They want to become runners because it is the only chance to acquire wealth and make a reputation since going into politics is only possible for the rich. In Kenya, four out of five people are living in the countryside at an altitude of 1,500m or higher where yearround the temperatures are between 20 and 28 °C – ideal conditions for running. Most Kenyan world-class athletes are from the agricultural highlands in the West of the Rift Valley and the majority of them come from humble families. Even Paul Tergat often went hungry as a child. Nowadays he is a multimillionaire and a role model for a whole generation.

How old is athletics? Running over long distances to deliver messages, running fast to escape or running to hunt, jumping over obstacles or rivers, throwing an implement to defend themselves or hunting an animal are altogether natural forms of physical exercises related to the environment and the daily routine of the natives in Africa. Physical exercises were and still are part of traditional dances and cultural events. In the rural parts of Kenya, even in the 21st century, they still play an important part. Visitors from the Western hemisphere are always impressed by the rhythm of movement and the natural flexibility of African performers.

Tea plantations around Kericho

At the beginning of the 20th century, many British settled in Kenya and in a short time they became wealthy with their huge tea and coffee plantations. In the course of the years, the colonial power then brought sport to Kenya. Golf, tennis, cricket, horse racing and polo were the sports for the white elite, while soccer, boxing and other athletics were left to the locals. Initially, African sport was concentrated in the Armed Forces (army, police). Later, there were colonial championships and even "inter territorial" meetings with neighboring Uganda. When Kenya became independent in December 1963, it had already participated in two Olympic Games: Melbourne 1956 and Rome 1960. It was Wilson Kiprugut who won the first medal for his country, a bronze in the 800 meters at the 1964 games in Tokyo. Four years later in Mexico, Kenya was celebrating its first Olympic gold medals won by Taftali Temu and Kipchoge Keino.

Nairobi in the year 2006

The first Kenyan government under President Jomo Kenyatta reformed the school system, and it was at that time when the sport entered secondary schools – a goldmine for scouts. It wasn't last long before American colleges became aware of the English-speaking Kenyan running talent. Such athletes as Sammy Koskei, Paul Ereng, Peter Rono, Peter Koech, Julius Kariuki, Ibrahim Hussein, Yobes Ondieki and Patrick Sang went to U.S. universities and managed to reach the top while they were there in the eighties, Mike Boit already ten years earlier. During that period, the international athletics federation dispensed with its antiquated amateur rules.

More and more Kenyans realized that in Europe and the USA it was possible to make a living on running.

As more athletes were able to build nice houses or buy farms after their trips to the "Promised Land" and managed to run away from poverty, the more young children wanted to emulate them. There is no country in the world that produces so many world-class athletes than Kenya.

Only a few runners are from the ethnic groups of the Turkanas (Paul Ereng, Olympic Champion at 800m in 1988) or Kikuyus (Julius Kariuki, Olympic Champion at 3,000m steeplechase in 1988). The vast majority are Kalenjins (Nandi, Kipsigis, Keiyo, Marakwet, Tugen, West Pokot), even though the Kalenjins amount to only 12 percent of the total population. Why is that so? Some say that God chose the Kalenjins as his "running people." Others see it in a more pragmatic light and refer to their genetic advantages.

KENYA'S LAST 150 YEARS

Around 1850	Researchers and missionaries follow the caravan routes to Uganda. In 1846, Krapf and Rebmann set up the first mission at Rabai. Twelve years later, Burton and Speke reach Lake Victoria.
1873	Bargash bin Said, the sultan of Zanzibar, prohibits the slave trade in his territory.
1884/85	At the conference in Berlin, the United Kingdom and Germany discuss their colonial rights. The area of today's states, Uganda and Kenya, becomes the British sphere of influence.

	It is agreed as to how East Africa is going to be divided.
1885	The beginning of East Africa's colonial rule. Kenya becomes a protectorate as British East Africa.
1896-1901	The British construct the Uganda railway. Nairobi is founded as a camp for railroaders.
1920	The British East African protectorate is declared the Kenyan Colony. The coast strip that belongs to the sultan of Zanzibar gets subordinated as a Kenyan protectorate under the rule of the British.
1952-1956	A revolt of the Mau-Mau movement.
1963	Kenya gains independence.
1964	Kenya becomes a republic with Jomo Kenyatta as the first president.
1978	After Kenyatta's death, Daniel arap Moi takes over as the new head of state.
1982	The government prevents a coup d'état by the Air Force.
2002	Mwai Kibaki wins the elections against Kenyatta's son, Uhuru, and becomes Kenya's third president.
2006	Total population 33 million people, among them 42.5% are between 0 and 14 years old, only 2.3% are 65 and older.

*Competing
for keeping fit
is still a rarity*

RUNNING AWAY FROM POVERTY

A few figures from the CIA Factbook:

- 15% of Kenyans older than 15 years old are not able to write or read

- 50% of the population lives under the poverty line

- The poorest 10% share 2% of the household income, the richest 10% have 37.2%

- 40% are jobless

- The average life expectancy is 48 years

- 75% of the population are in the agricultural sector, many are self-sufficient

They all have the same vision: They want to run away from poverty. But not all succeed in getting there. Many former top-class athletes from Kenya didn't make anything out of their fame – or couldn't make anything.

Charles Asati was the 1972 Olympic Champion with the Kenyan relay team in Munich. He was also twice Commonwealth Champion at 400m. More than 30 years later Asati still lives at Iringa, a godforsaken dump in the Nyanza Province in the West of the country. He depends on alms. He is bitter when he thinks about the past. It is hard for him to accept his fate. "I really feel very bad when I see how much money the best athletes are getting these days in an event I was dominating in my time."

Kenya's first Olympic champion, Naftali Temu, was poor when he died in a Nairobi hospital in 2003, almost unnoticed by the general public and the Kenyan athletics fraternity. Of all the athletes of the first generation, Kipchoge Keino is the only one who managed to transform his successes on the track into fame and fortune.

Samson Kimobwa, Kenya's first World Record holder at 10,000m in 1977, was on the stage of world athletics for only a summer. Today, he is an ordinary primary school teacher with a monthly income of about $ 200 US, and beside that he is a small provincial coach. His successor, the great Henry Rono who broke four World Records in 1978 within only 80 days, became an alcoholic. For years, he fought his way as a car washer in the American town of Portland. At least now he has a job as an assistant coach, but after all his negative press he doesn't dare return to his native Kenya.

And then there was Richard Chelimo, the biggest long distance talent of the early nineties. He was World Junior Champion 1990 in the 10,000m. A year later – at only 19 years old, he was second at the World Championships. In 1992 he won an Olympic silver medal and at 21 he became the World Record holder. By the time he was 23 his career came to an end. It is said that his love of chang'aa, the high-proof local brew, was stronger than his will to become one of the all time greats. On Aug. 15, 2001, Richard Chelimo passed away. The official cause of death: brain tumor. The unofficial cause: HIV, the deadly virus that – depending on the source – between 7 and 12 percent of all adults in Kenya carry.

Nine months before his death, I was visiting Chelimo at Chesubet in the Cherangani Hills, a small farm in no man's land where there is no electricity, running water, or sewage system.

Richard Chelimo

There he lived a secluded live with his wife and their three kids. Richard Chelimo was just coming back from the local bar when I arrived. He looked 40 with his bloated face and bloodshot eyes, yet he was only 28.

But the positive examples are in a majority. Julius Kariuki, steeplechase Olympic Champion 1988 in Seoul, is the "ruler of Moi's Bridge", a proprietor of a hotel and the biggest pharmacy in town, as well as a big landowner. Peter Rono, who won the 1,500m in Seoul, completed his studies in economics at Mount St. Mary's College in Maryland (Washington D.C.) with a master's degree and is now working as a coach in the USA, the same as then-800-meters Olympic Champion, Paul Ereng. In 1996, Daniel Komen still lived in a hut without water and electricity. Now he is the proud owner of a villa worth 12 million Ksh, approximately $160,000 US – not a big deal for somebody who earned a quarter million dollars with just his Grand Prix overall and event victory in 1996.

Julius Kariuki with the diploma from the Seoul Olympics

Most of the top athletes of modern times, some of them millionaires, have in recent years settled down at Eldoret, about 320 kilometers northwest of Nairobi. They can afford to. They belong to the financial elite of the country. At the same time, they are the ones forcing up the prices for real estate by putting almost every amount on the table without batting an eyelid. For example, Moses Kiptanui and Sammy Korir have erected big shopping and business centers in the town.

Moses Kiptanui's building in the center of Eldoret

Ibrahim Hussein, the marathon king of the eighties with wins in Honolulu, New York and Boston (two), has, beside the obligatory farm, a four-story building with apartments and shops. There, he runs a billiard bar and a shop for exclusive goods imported from Dubai. In the national federation, "Athletics Kenya," Hussein is the deputy General Secretary.

Patrick Sang, the Kenyan coordinator for Jos Hermens' "Global Sports Communication," graduated in the U.S. as a city planner. He invested his money in real estate and is also the owner of a pharmacy. From his time as a world-class athlete he still has his personal financial adviser in Zurich. You don't have to worry about him or Yobes Ondieki for that matter. Ondieki was the first man to break the 27-minute barrier in the 10,000m. He owns different rental houses and is a partner of a gym with state-of-the-art equipment. At the same time, he is coaching a group of athletes. As with Hussein, Rono, Ereng and Sang, Ondieki belongs to the generation that didn't only concentrate on the sport, but went with scholarships to the U.S. and completed their studies. Today, it's paying off.

Paul Tergat is probably the wealthiest of all of them. A five-time World Cross-country Champion and multiple World Record holder on the track and on the road, he picked up a cool $ 300,000 US appearance money, just for his first marathon in 2001 in London. In the course of the years, he has raked in several millions. In Nairobi, he is operating an office with ten employees who take care of his different businesses. Tergat has a farm with about 16 hectares at Turbo in the northwest of the country and at Kabarak near Nakuru in the direct neighborhood of former President Daniel arap Moi he has another one with 32 hectares. Tergat bought and built houses at his residence Ngong and in Nairobi, a hotel in his home district Baringo, and he is the owner and publisher of the only athletics magazine in East Africa. He holds different shares and is active on the stock exchange.

Lest it be forgotten, he also comes from a very poor family. There were 17 children together with all the half-brothers and half-sisters; his father had three wives. Sometimes there was nothing to eat. Later, when he joined secondary school, his parents could not afford to pay the school fees. But Tergat didn't want to stay at home. He knew that education is the key to everything. So he asked the teacher to waive the fees for the time being and assured him that he would refund everything as soon as he earned his first money. The headmaster agreed. The rest is history.

What running away from poverty means can also be illustrated with the example of Chemokil Chilapong. Grinding poverty forced her out of class seven following the death of her mother. She married early at 18 years old, and for the next nine years she lived the normal life of a rural young wife caring for her four children and husband. But she never gave up her old passion, which was running. She was running every day and dreaming of becoming an international athlete. At the end of 2004, her coach, Wilfred Lorot, encouraged her to enter for the Nairobi Marathon. Chemokil's husband, Benjamin, had to sell a sheep and a chicken to make it possible the two to travel 500 kilometers by bus to the capital city.

There, something happened that Chemokil Chilapong could

not have even imagined in her wildest dreams. She defeated the internationally renowned Joyce Chepchuma, won the marathon and received a prize of one million Ksh, equivalent to almost $ 14,000 US. To show how much this is, a painter has to work at least eight years to earn this amount of money.

Since that victory, Chilapong has risen from a small-scale potato farmer to the proud owner of a five-acre plot in Kapenguria town. The plot is being developed into a residential estate. Her husband who used to buy and sell goats at the local market, now buys and transports cows to Nairobi and other big towns.

Chemokil Chilapong, proud owner of a new home

In Kenya, even in the 21st century, fairy tales sometimes become reality.

DO THEY HAVE GENETIC ADVANTAGES?

Since 1960, Ethiopian athletes have won 31 Olympic medals, Kenyans have won 54, despite the fact that both countries were boycotting several Olympics: the two East African long distance giants were not present in 1976, Kenya again in 1980, Ethiopia in 1984 and again in 1988. The world list shows that Kenyan male athletes are dominating all distances from 800 meters to marathon (see the statistics at the end of the book). What are the secrets behind these facts? What are the explanations? Are the young boys and girls driven by socio-cultural aspects, like poverty, looking for recognition and the fact that there is a tradition and a culture when it comes to running in Kenya? There is no doubt that these factors are important. But why do the majority of the top runners live in a geographically narrow area? Why are at least three-fourths of the Kenyan world-class athletes from the Kalenjin tribe? It is difficult not to think of genetic advantages.

For many years, scientists from all over the world tried to find reasons for the Kenyan superiority in long distance running. These days, they have ruled out most of the popular explanations. Given the fact that most of the East African runners live at an altitude between 1,800 and 2,400 meters above sea level, many scientists thought that this could be the main factor. At these altitudes, there is an increase in red blood cells, which are responsible for oxygen transport in the muscles. But scientists have found altitude is not the key to the riddle. There is no difference between Kenyan and other world-class athletes in their capacity to consume oxygen. And the Kenyan diet is nothing special beside the fact that they don't eat a lot of meat and have a very high carbohydrate intake compared with Americans or Europeans (see the chapter about eating habits).

Is there a gene that favors endurance? The differences in physique and muscle make-up that underline the dominance of Kenyan endurance runners and West African sprinters doubtless have a strong genetic component. Various studies have shown that West African athletes have denser bones, less body fat, narrower hips, thicker thighs, longer legs, and lighter calves than whites. But the differences between East and West Africans are even more striking. The Kenyan runners are small, thin and tend to weigh between 50 and 60 kilograms, whereas West African athletes are taller and a good 30 kilograms heavier. The differences don't stop with body shape; there is also evidence of a difference in the predominant types of muscle fibers.

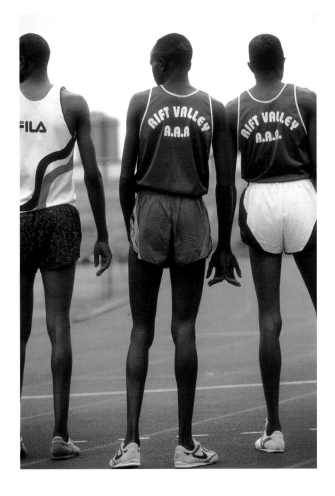

An average person has 50 percent slow muscle fibers and 50 percent fast ones. West Africans have many more type II or fast-twitch fibers; East Africans have many more type I or slow-twitch fibers. There is evidence that, with extremely intensive long-distance training, fast fibers can change to slow fibers, up to a level of 90 percent. So far, however, there is no evidence that slow-twitch fibers can be turned into fast-twitch ones. Do Kenyan runners have a higher percentage of slow-twitch fibers than other world-class athletes? The answer is no. Muscle biopsies show that there is no difference. In other words, the secret has to be found elsewhere.

Running to school – even in the 21st century

Researchers are only just getting off the starting blocks in the search for genes that influence running performance. Yannis Pitsiladis of the University of Glasgow's Institute of Biomedical and Life Science has spent the past few years in searching for a special "running gene." Asked about the findings at the end of 2005, his answer was vague, the results still not convincing. "The latest is that we have not discovered one yet, maybe because they don't possess one? Our work continues, however, as there are some 30,000 genes we have to go through...In years to come, we are sure it will be proved that if you don't have the right genes then you won't be a top athlete. What we'll also discover is that it will be the same genes making East African runners successful as those that make Paula Radcliffe a winner. If you don't choose your parents carefully, you'll never be one of the best."

In 2001, then-World Anti-Doping Agency chairman Richard Pound said, "The kind of people who cheat in sport today will probably try to find ways to misuse genetics tomorrow." Gene transfer technology – currently being developed as a tool for battling debilitating illnesses and deficiencies – is said to have the potential for just such abuse. According to some experts, a so-called performance gene could not only be isolated, but the technology then used to replace or modify someone's genetic pattern in order to substantially improve an individual's capability – without detection. Nevermind the soy beans, what about genetically modified athletes?

In this context a very provoking thesis comes from Andy Miah, author of "Genetically Modified Athletes: Biomedical Ethics, Gene Doping and Sport." The prospect of a future of genetically modified athletes incites alarm throughout the sports world, accompanied by portrayals of such athletes as inhuman or some form of mutant. This is a misinterpretation of how gene transfer would alter humans, should it ever be legalized. But the fear that rogue scientists will take advantage of athletes – or that athletes will seek to enroll in gene-transfer experiments in an attempt to receive some undetectable performance benefit – is very real.

The World Anti-Doping Agency prohibited gene doping in 2003, but some scientists predict that its misuse in sport is likely to appear at the Bejing 2008 Olympics.

"The rhetoric surrounding 'gene doping' relies heavily on its moral status as a form of cheating. Yet, this status relies on existing anti-doping rules. If we don't ban gene transfer in the first place, then on one level, it is not cheating … After all, many if not most, top athletes are 'naturally' genetically gifted. To refer to these people as mutants would surely invite widespread criticism.

"Those who fear that gene doping heralds the 'end of sports' should instead recognize this moment as an opportunity to ask critical questions about the effectiveness and validity of anti-doping tests. Does society really care about performance enhancement in sport?" Miah asks. A very controversial and even frightening standpoint, indeed.

In any case, there is a gene called ACE (Angiotensis Converting Enzyme), found by British scientists in 1998, which is connected to the endurance performance of a human being. This "endurance gene" influences the blood circulation's control mechanism in the muscles. Scientists discovered that mountaineers who were able to move even at a height of 7,000 meters without the help of additional oxygen have a special composition of this gene.

So what about Kenyan runners? An important clue is the ability to resist fatigue longer. Lactic acid, generated by tired, oxygen-deprived muscles, accumulates slower in their blood. Comparisons of lactate levels have suggested to the group of Bengt Saltin from the Muscle Research Center in Copenhagen that Kenyan runners squeeze about 10 percent more mileage from the same oxygen intake than Europeans.

Just as more aerodynamic cars get better gas mileage, the Kenyan physiology helps explain their fuel efficiency. The Kalenjin possess birdlike legs, which are thin and long. Saltin's group with Henrik Larsen and Hans Södergaard has quantified this observation. Compared with Danes, the thinner calves of Kenyans have, on average, 400 grams or 12 percent less flesh in each lower leg. According to the study, this explains why the running economy was found to be 10 percent better in the Kenyans. Apart from this fact, the Kenyans had relatively longer legs (5 percent), which is probably a result of the nomadic life these people were used to for generations at high altitude. To be able to move over great distances with low energy expenditure has been essential in order to survive.

Walking for hours and hours

Thinner legs means fewer muscles and this means less oxygen for muscles. The farther a weight is from the center of gravity, the more energy it takes to move it. Fifty grams added to the ankle will increase oxygen consumption by 1 percent. For the Kenyans, that translates into an 8 percent energy savings to run a kilometer. In other words, Kenyans are more efficient because it takes less energy to swing their limbs.

- Elite Kenyan runners were about 7cm shorter and about 5kg lighter than elite Danish runners. Furthermore, the body mass index of the Kenyan runners was substantially lower.

- Kenyan runners have a very high maximal oxygen uptake. However, the VO_2 max of the Kenyans was not higher compared to the Danish runners.

- Kenyan runners had lower plasma lactic acid concentrations at sub-maximal running speeds, also when related to oxygen uptake.

- No difference in muscle fiber composition was observed. There were, however, some distinct differences in the muscle enzyme profile. The activity of the HAD enzyme (3-hydroxyacyl CoA dehydrogenase) was markedly higher in the muscles of the Kenyan runners indicating that they have a better ability to utilize fat while running.

- Elite Kenyan runners had a better running economy. Since elite Kenyan runners are more slender than elite Danish runners, they run faster at a given energy production per kg of body weight. In addition, Kenyans have thinner lower legs. The lower leg thickness is a crucial factor for running economy.

The scientists drew the conclusion that the optimal body shape of a distance runner with respect to running economy is a combination of small height, slender body shape and thin lower legs.

None of the data from the various studies negate the importance of cultural habits and training. The Kenyans train harder and more than other runners – also their bodies can bear more than those of most of the athletes in the Western world. Paul Tergat didn't have an injury for twelve years, and he is not an exception. But the fact remains: Differences among athletes of elite caliber are so small that if you have an advantage that might be genetically based, it could be very significant.

If it is true that mankind survived and stood out against other creatures because of its ability to run over long distances, does it mean that the Kenyan super-runners are human beings made and prepared for an easy survival in the future? Could they be more privileged? Or are the East Africans because of their almost unchanged way of life over thousands of years only nearer at the origin of mankind than we children of the affluent society?

THE SCIENCE OF KENYAN EATING

When Paul Tergat was asked about his eating habits, his answer came quite surprisingly: "I have never taken any food supplements in my life, not even vitamins. Maybe the food in Europe and in the USA is not as balanced and fresh as what we eat in Kenya and, therefore, athletes in those countries have to add these supplements. I usually go for an annual general check-up to find out if there is any substance in my body missing or under the required level. But I never had a problem."

As we mentioned before, most of the Kenyan athletes come from poor families. In other words, for almost their first 20 years of life their food is very simple but healthy. In a rural Kenyan home, you might get meat only once every one or two weeks. Sugar is only found in the tea (Chai). The food intake only changes when they go to a national camp, e.g., for the World Cross-country Championships, where they get meat twice a day, and when they get in touch with french fries or hamburgers in Europe or the USA.

Basic Kenyan food contains all the body needs:

Carbohydrates: Ugali (a thick mash made out of boiled white corn/maize meal and water, at least once a day), Chapati (looks like an omelette but is prepared only with flour and water), Uji (millet or corn/maize porridge) and Viazi (potatoes)

Iron and minerals: Sukuma Wiki (a kind of spinach) and other vegetables

Protein: Maziwa (milk), Maziwa Lala (fermented milk) and Maharagwe (beans)

Vitamins: Matunda (fruits, especially green oranges, bananas, mangos and papaya)

A world-class athlete like Paul Tergat eats most of these traditional foods but also has pasta, rice and meat on his menu. He drinks tea, fruit juices, water and, from time to time, a soda.

Does it mean the Kenyan athletes instinctively eat the right stuff? To answer this and other questions, researchers from the International Centre for East African Running Science monitored everything that went in the mouth of ten elite Kenyan runners over a seven-day period at the Global Sports training camp near Kaptagat. All ten runners belonged to the Kalenjin tribe. Two of the athletes specialized in 1,500m running, the others were training for 8 and 12km cross-country competitions. Their mean height was 1.75 meters, their body weight averaging 58.6 kilograms and their body fat ranging from 6 to 10 percent.

The ten athletes followed their normal diets and weighed and recorded everything that was consumed (both food and drink). They ate five times a day, according to the following plan:

Breakfast at 8:00

Mid-morning snack at 10:00

Lunch at 13:00

Afternoon snack at 16:00

Supper at 19:00

Most of their nutrients came from vegetable sources, the "staple" edibles being bread, boiled rice, poached potatoes, boiled porridge, cabbage, kidney beans and ugali. Meat – primarily beef – was taken in just four times per week in fairly small amounts (about 100 grams per day). Naturally, a fair amount of tea with milk and sugar was imbibed on a daily basis. None of these ten top-class athletes was taking any kind of supplements.

About 86 percent of their daily calories came from vegetable sources, with 14 percent from animal foods. The Kenyan runners' diet was very rich in carbohydrates, comprising 76.5 percent of daily calories. They were ingesting about 10.4 grams of carbohydrates per kilogram of body mass each day. An amazing fact was their consistency: every 24 hours, they took in about 600 grams of carbohydrate, with very little variation from day to day. They were truly stocking their muscles with glycogen. Incidentally, sports-nutrition experts frequently recommend that athletes involved in strenuous training should consume at least 9 grams of carbohydrates per kilogram of body mass per day, so these Kenyan top athletes were eating according to current scientific data.

Breakfast after the early morning run: bread, margarine or butter and "chai"

Their fat intake was found to be modest: about 13.4 percent of daily calories came from fat (approximatly 46 grams), with 61 percent of these calories coming from milk. Protein intake amounted to 10.1 percent of all calories and a total of 1.3 grams of protein per kilogram of body weight per day (75 grams daily).

Once again the athletes were fully in line with recommendations by sports nutritionists, who call for protein intakes of approximately 1.2 grams per kilogram daily for endurance athletes. About two-thirds of the protein came from plant foods. Water intake was modest: about 1.113 liters per day, and the athletes actually tended to drink more tea than water; the daily tea consumption simmered at about 1.243 liters.

As one might expect, the national dish ugali furnished about 23 percent of the runners' daily calories. In second position there was surprisingly "the bad" sugar with 20 percent – about 133 grams a day! Let's not forget: As long as the rest of the diet is rich in vitamins, minerals, fibers and anti-oxidants, and as long as calorie intake does not exceed calorie expenditure, sugar is not a bad thing at all. In addition  to taking in slightly more than the amount of daily carbohydrates that are recommended for athletes, the Kenyans also used another fundamental principle of sports nutrition to enhance their abilities to train and perform well. That is they always ate within one hour after workouts. When carbohydrate ingestion is delayed after a training session, lower total intramuscular glycogen levels are often the result.

According to the ICEARS study, the daily carbohydrate intake of elite distance runners in the United States and the Netherlands have been measured at 49 and 50 percent of total calories, a far cry from the Kenyan total of 76.5 percent. The Kenyans appear to do a far better job in fueling themselves for their very demanding training.

CORRUPTION IN KENYA'S SPORT

As in most African countries, corruption is still a major problem in Kenyan society. A lot has remained untouched even though the new president, Mwai Kibaki, who took over at the end of 2002 after 24 years of the Moi regime, declared war on the country's main plague and established an anti-corruption-office. Policemen still let traffic offenders go if they are willing to fork something out, and in many offices you can speed up processes if you give a helping hand.

On a regular basis, Kenyan newspapers report on embezzled public funds and on land that is acquired illegally or taken

Here was the KAAA office in the nineties

over by members of the political caste. Millions, if not billions, of tax payers' money and dollars from international organizations disappear every year into politicians' pockets or private bank accounts in Switzerland or elsewhere. Some might say the new government proves good intention, but talking is not enough. It might take generations until this basic evil is eliminated from the African reality.

Koigi Wa Wamwere, a critical politician and member of the parliament, who by the way is from the same party as President Kibaki, wrote in an article in the "Daily Nation," Kenya's leading newspaper: "When President Kibaki was elected, he promised to fight corruption, win or die. But the war on corruption never began. In Kenya, besides robbing and fleecing the poor, corruption has divided society into victims and beneficiaries. As a beneficiary, the President will only fight corruption superficially. He has benefited from inequitable distribution of land and national income that has made him and others wealthy landlords while consigning millions to destitution. Recently, budgetary corruption gave the President's district hundreds of millions of shillings for roads and water while more deserving districts got nothing. The country lacks a President who has the courage to fire his ministers for becoming billionaires over night."

In a country where bribery and corruption are a part of everyday life, even sport is not untouched. I still remember in 1992 when Paul Tergat won his first national title in cross-country, and had to pull out from the World Championships in Boston because of an injury. He asked me to invite him to Switzerland. Several times I called David Okeyo who at that time was the federation's secretary. But his answer was always the same: Tergat must not travel abroad.

A few months later Tergat appeared in Italy. It seems that "Dottore" Gabriele Rosa was smarter than me and accompanied his request probably with some "chai" – which a bribe is called in Kenya.

In the early '90s, Okeyo worked as a press officer for the national railway company, but nevertheless within a few years managed to own a beautiful house in Nairobi and had enough money to send his daughter for schooling in Paris. Undoubtedly, his job at the federation and all the connections to the athlete's agents contributed fundamentally to his wealth. Yobes Ondieki, once the top athlete, recalls, "In the early '90s the federation wanted 5% from all our income, but we athletes fought successfully against it. I am certain that some agents were paying the federation for getting good athletes."

"Athletics Kenya" is one of the few sports federations in the country that is well off. However, one doesn't see a lot of change from their 60 million Ksh annual income – more than $ 800,000 US. There is a competition series during the cross-country season and one at the beginning of the track season, there are national training camps before World Championships and Olympic Games, but there is no program for recruiting and developing the talents, and there is no national coaching structure. According to Colm O'Connell, coach of Isaac Songok and Augustine Choge, there was not even one representative of the federation asking about the athletes, let alone visiting one of their trainings between the World Cross-country Championships 2005 in France or the World Championships five months later in Helsinki. And let's not forget that Choge was the Junior World Champion and Songok the bronze medal winner in the short cross at the time.

So where does the money go? In the pockets of some officials? "The Standard," the number two newspaper in the country, quoted a senior member of the Ministry for Sports saying that many officials would try to get their expenses and allowances three times; first from the government, then from the national federation and eventually from the international body. Questions were raised as to how it was possible that in 2004

"Athletics Kenya" was spending 4.1 million Ksh (approximately $ 55,000 US) for a five-day trip to the African Championships in Congo Brazzaville and about $ 65,000 US for the team to the World Junior Championships in the Italian town of Grosseto. Following the article in "The Standard," in both cases more than half of the money went as allowances in the officials' accounts.

According to an "AK" insider, of the money the federation gets from its sponsor, Nike, every year, $ 25,000 US goes directly to the account of the chairman, and 18,000 each goes to the secretary and treasurer.

Another story that made headlines during the World Championships 2005 in Helsinki fits well in this context. A part of Kenya's official uniform for the national team was found to be on sale in sports and other shops in Nairobi. Kip Keino, chairman of the National Olympic Committee, was speechless. "These are track suits for the athletics federation. Not long ago we were delivering four lorries." It seems that an employee of "Athletics Kenya" has found a lucrative side income, and, not for the first time: Before the Olympic Games 1996 in Atlanta official track suits appeared in the "Nairobi Sports House."

"It came into fashion in Europe to blame all imaginable negative attributes on the Africans." Julius Nyerere, Tanzania's first president, was very indignant when he expressed his feelings some time ago. "We are said to be corrupt, lazy, hopeless and unpredictable. But it was you people who decided Africa's destiny 70 of the last 100 years. Certainly we have made mistakes in the 30 years since our independence. But are we therefore the only ones responsible for all that goes wrong these days on this continent?"

ALL POWER TO THE MANAGERS

The Kenyan athletics federation has failed to remain in control of its athletes. Today, agents have the power.

Athletics Kenya carries out the selections for international championships and takes care of the athletes on the spot – and that's all more or less. The agents are the ones to decide together with the athletes and the meet organizers who will run where and when. Before the World Championships in 2005 it worked like that. When the trials for Helsinki were over, the chairman of Athletics Kenya, Isaiah Kiplagat, announced that all selected athletes had to report in Nairobi for a four-week training camp. Races abroad would only be possible after consulting the federation but would not in any case be allowed for the last two weeks. These were strong words from a man who is in office until 2008 but now has few supporters.

AK chairman Isaiah Kiplagat

It brought back some bad memories. In 2001, the Kenyan federation made an example of and dropped Noah Ngeny, reigning Olympic 1,500m Champion from the previous year, and marathon runner Tegla Loroupe from the World Championships' team because they didn't return in time from Europe. In the run-up to Helsinki, this scenario was not likely to be repeated. The athletes' agents are a stronger force these days.

They are well aware of their importance. They were the ones who were establishing camps in the country and who are still spending a lot of money on developing young talents. And so came what was to be expected. Only a few athletes trained in Nairobi, the majority remained with their home coaches and traveled all over Europe at their own discretion.

Athletics Kenya could probably only keep its athletes at home if the loss of earnings could be compensated. Running is a profession. That means a runner has to try making as much money as possible in a few years. A career can be over at any time. If he does it without the lucrative starts in Europe, he might lose quite a lot. One should know that Kenyan athletes don't get any financial support from the athletics federation or the national sports authority. There are no funds for the actual or former athletes. All the money an athlete earns, he gets via his agent from his appearances and prize money, as well as commercial contracts. The 300,000 Ksh, approximately $ 4,000 US, which were paid by the National Olympic Committee for a gold medal in Athens, are peanuts compared to the $ 250,000 US the federation of Qatar promised its athletes.

In Ethiopia, the situation is a little bit different. Until recently, an athlete was only allowed to leave the country with the authorization of the national federation and the government. Recently, this iron grip has been slightly loosened, and it has yet to be seen how this will affect future performances at the Olympic Games and World Championships.

For 20 years, Kenyan athletes always prepared together in a training camp for several weeks before a big international event. The camps at the Kigari Teacher's College at the foot of Mount Kenya in the run-up of the World Cross-country

Championships are legendary. It was there that not only the athlete's shape was sharpened but tactical plans were hatched. Mike Kosgei who was Kenya's national coach for 15 years was a master in this field. In the end, even for him, it became more and more difficult as fewer runners were ready to sacrifice themselves for one another. The national team was not the main thing but success for Adidas, Nike or whichever personal sponsor was involved. The national coach, most recently Dan Muchoki, had lost his influence. In contrast to Ethiopia, where all the effort is concentrated in Addis Ababa and where national coach Dr. Woldemeskel Kostre can see his people almost on a daily basis, the top athletes in Kenya are in different training groups at Eldoret, Iten, Kaptagat, Kapsait, Kapsabet, Nairobi and Ngong.

Gianni Demadonna (on the right) is one of the most influential agents

In Kenya, the running scene has changed dramatically in the past 30 years. First, the Armed Forces were the main employers for the runners, later came other public institutions, such as the Prison Administration and the Kenyan Postal Services. They still play a certain role. Three of the best female athletes of the country, Catherine Ndereba, Edith Masai and Margaret Okayo, belong to the Prisons Services and Paul Tergat, Sammy Kipketer or John Kibowen to the Armed Forces. At the national championships where the team competition always plays an important role, the athletes compete in the colors of their local employers, but at the same time they belong to Global Sports, Rosa & Associati, Demadonna Athletics, Spear Sports Management or Kimbia Athletics.

All these agencies maintain one or more training camps in the country. Normally these camps are rental houses, in some cases they are built only for this purpose. In most of these "camps" a European or American athlete would not last even two weeks because everything is very, very simple. "Dottore" Rosa's Nike camp at Kapsait in the Cherangani Hills at 3,000m above sea level is one example why. Here, where the world ends, there is space for 100 athletes, but there is no electricity, no running water and no network for mobile phones. The athlete's life consists of training, eating, sleeping.

Rosa's idea was to gather many athletes in the same place and teach them not only the training methods but also a lifestyle so that they can become authentic professional runners. "It is necessary to dedicate all day to the training program," Rosa says. The schedule of the day is always the same:

6:30 a.m.:	morning training
9:00 a.m.:	breakfast
10:00 a.m.:	relax or personal activities
12:30 p.m.:	lunch
2:30 p.m.:	relax
4:30 p.m.:	second training
7:30 p.m.:	supper
9:30 p.m.:	sleep

This kind of timetable does not only set the course of the day but also the way of life. The athletes who join are obligated to leave their families, friends and jobs for many months.

Foreigners like the "Dottore" from Italy have a strong grip on athletics in Kenya. Even the different defections, especially to Qatar and Bahrain that started in August 2003 with Stephen Cherono are a strong indication that Athletics Kenya is not doing enough for its athletes. When Cherono, a.k.a Saif Saaeed Shaheen, was asked why he decided to replace his Kenyan passport with the Qatari one, his answer was clear and unmistakable: "In the course of the years I have seen that Kenya is not supporting its athletes at all and former world-beaters at times die like animals because there is nobody who cares about them. I want to be spared this fate."

Mike Boit, at that time the commissioner for sports, and David Okeyo in the early nineties

National Cross-country Championships 2005 at 12km, on the right Eliud Kipchoge

Sir Derek Erskine
(on the right)

PART 2:
THE MEN WHO MADE
KENYANS RUN

THE PIONEERS IN THE FIFTIES AND SIXTIES

Let's take you back to the 1950s. Kenya was at that time a colony and the whole country was racially divided. A European would have lived in a European quarter in Nairobi, next door to Asians. The Africans had a few settlements on the edge of the city. The schools were segregated, and a European boy would have gone to a European school; they were among the very best in the Commonwealth. The Asians had their own schools. Taking that one step further, when the boy left school he would join a European club, the Asians the Asian clubs. For Africans, there were no clubs. So what they had to rely on was the program that was put together by the colony sports officers.

Furthermore, to maintain colonial order, the British believed that they should not prepare Africans to compete against Europeans, lest the Africans forget "their place" in the colonial hierarchy. Absolute rule required absolute separatism. If soldiers or schoolboys were encouraged to run or play football, it was to help them only to compete against other Africans. The only contact the people of Kenya had with upper-class games like golf or tennis were as caddies, custodians of golf courses, and ball boys.

During the colonial period, the British Government had assigned Archie Evans to be a sports officer in charge of all the sports programs in Kenya. Mal Whitfield describes him in his book "Beyond the Finish Line" "Evans was a slim but muscular 160-pound athlete. Because he seldom wore a cap, his face had been baked tomato-red from the Nairobi sun, which burns even more intensely at an altitude of 5,800 feet above sea level.

"When attending any official function, Evans always wore a tweed jacket, and was never without a proper tie. Also, in typical British fashion, he always carried a briefcase with him everywhere during business hours. He was the epigone of a colonial employee – very correct, with a positive attitude and outlook as befitted a subject of the British Crown. Evans, however, was simply following a protocol which had been initiated during the 19th century, when the British took over the 1,000 year old spice and slave track from the Arabs."

Evans' office was at Kabete outside Nairobi at the Kenya Institute of Administration. At the same time, he was the national athletics coach until 1964. When Kenya sent its first teams to the 1956 Olympic Games in Melbourne and the 1960 Games in Rome, Archie Evans was the Athletics Manager and Reggie S. Alexander headed the delegation as the chairman of the Kenyan Olympic Association. The KOA, the forerunner to the National Olympic Committee of Kenya (NOCK), was founded in 1954 by Alexander, who was to lead it for the next

14 years. At its formation, KOA's main responsibility was to enter teams in the Commonwealth and Olympic Games.

The first chairman of the Kenyan Amateur Athletics Association, K.A.A.A., which was established in 1951, was  Sir Derek Erskine. Like Reggie S. Alexander, Erskine was a business man. He had become a very successful entrepreneur and rancher and he was a very wealthy person, so he was able to put some money into athletics. The whole area where Nyayo Stadium now stands was donated by him. He was a very active man and instrumental in the fight in getting Kenya's first head of state, Jomo Kenyatta, out of prison. It was for this that he was eventually knighted by the Queen. Erskine was chairman of K.A.A.A. until one year after independence. In Kenya, he contributed vastly to sport and the idea of racial equality. Everyone was always welcomed at his dining room table – Africans, whites and Asians alike.

Reggie S. Alexander

Before independence, Kenya was divided into provinces, districts and locations. Right from the very bottom, from the chief upwards, there was a structure put in place. It was a typical structure that would have been found in any other British colony at that time. When there was a national championship in athletics, it would start from the very bottom. The chiefs would organize small village athletics meets, and they would then move up the scale to the districts.

From there, the best got to the provincial level and later to the national championships. This structure not only served athletics and other sports, it served everything else, and it worked.

In the fifties, athletics was already a strong sport in Kenya. For the natives, there was also netball and volleyball, because they were cheap. However, soccer was the king of all sports. It dominated everything, budget-wise and facility-wise, and in support there were all sorts of cup competitions. Second to soccer but some distant way behind was athletics.

Kenya gained its independence on December 12, 1963, and a year later there was a total shift in authority and power. The newly independent state began to view sports as a means of developing nationalism and increasing national prestige. The transformation from a country that was a total colony in every sense of the word to an independent country with its own identity, its own national anthem, its own flag all happened in a very short period of time. Now the first multi-racial school came to Nairobi when the Delamare Boys School changed its name to Upper Hill School and accommodated an equal number of Europeans, Asians and Kenyans.

When independence came, many British had to leave the country, including Archie Evans, the tough colonial sports officer. However, John Velzian stayed. Velzian had come in 1959 and played an important role in developing athletics in Kenya. Almost half a century later, and remarkably youthful, he is still a driving force. He is the director of the IAAF regional development center in Nairobi and the race director for the Nairobi marathon. He has also been at the forefront for the bid to get the IAAF World Cross-country Championships in 2007 to Mombasa. Velzian came to Kenya by pure accident.

J. V. *"I was supposed to go to Cyprus as a director for outdoor sports. It didn't materialize because Cyprus was going to be divided. I had to report to the foreign office in London and there I was asked where else I would like to go. I said give me a weekend, I'll think about it. That weekend I went to the White City stadium where I saw two Kenyans running. So on Monday I went back and said: Can I go to Kenya? To be honest, I didn't even know whether Kenya was on the West coast or the East coast. But I had seen two great athletes. When I came to Kenya I was a bit of a misfit. So I worked in a school for a period of time."*

As the years went by, John Velzian did a lot of different things. He worked for the Ministry of Education and after attending a teacher training college, he was transferred as a lecturer to Nairobi University. He helped in the construction of stadiums and playing fields. In 1965, as a coach, he took Kenyan athletes to the first-ever African Championships in Congo Brazzaville. These games were very successful and laid the foundation for everything to come. When the team returned home, President Kenyatta himself met the athletes at the airport. They had a motorcade all the way to the city of Nairobi. One year later, Velzian returned from the Commonwealth Games in Jamaica with the first-ever Kenyan gold medals. It was the breakthrough for Kenyan athletics just two years before the Mexico Olympics.

John Velzian

John Velzian has remained involved in athletics in one way or another, as a coach, technical advisor or organizer of courses for coaches. He helped found the Kenyan Schools Athletics Association, which is one of the main sources for athletics talent in the country. The man who took over after him as the national head coach and led the team to the Mexico Olympics was Charles Mukora.

Mukora's name is synonymous with sports in his village Kagumo near Nyeri. He has the rare experience of having gone through all aspects of the sport as a competitor, a coach, a promoter, and an administrator to the IOC headquarters in Switzerland. In his youth, Mukora represented Kenya in both athletics and soccer. In athletics, he was on the Kenya team, which competed against Uganda, Tanzania and Ethiopia. He took part in long jump, triple jump and later the decathlon during the annual East African Championships. In soccer, he played in some of the major East African competitions.

Charles Mukora

Looking back, he pays tribute to his British teacher, John Cowley, who encouraged him to take up sport. After coming back from a one-year scholarship at the prestigious Loughborough College in England, Mukora was appointed as the deputy Kenya sports officer. He didn't stay long in that position before he was hired by Coca-Cola. Nevertheless, he was in charge of preparing the Kenyan team for the Olympic Games in Mexico City.

C. M. *"I selected Nyahururu as the training camp because the altitude was more or less the same as in Mexico. Previous to this, the team used to train at Kabete. We stayed at Nyahururu for one month. When I was the coach, I traveled quite a lot with the Kenyan athletes overseas. We were invited to many different countries for friendly competitions. It was very important because the athletes got to know the other strong competitors. They started to learn how they run and how they train. As a coach, you don't have to prepare the athlete only physically, but also mentally. You have to make him understand his race."*

"The training at Nyahururu was quite tough, three sessions a day with a lot of endurance and hill-work. We used a hill called 'agony hill'. The team was selected after the trials. They were the best athletes in the country. Nevertheless we had some people who almost collapsed when they got right to the top of 'agony hill'. People like Kip Keino and Taftali Temu were running up the hill many times. I put Keino in three events, the 1,500m, the 5,000m and the 10,000m because I knew how good he was. In Mexico we usually sacrificed the slowest in the race to run in front. We were running as a team. Tactics already played an important role. If you ask me, if I was surprised when Temu and Keino won their medals, I would answer: I was sure that not many people had trained as hard as our athletes."

Charles Mukora was still in charge at the Munich Olympics in 1972. Then he became the chairman of the athletics federation and Kip Keino took over as head coach. Mukora went even higher up the ladder. In 1976, he was elected to the IAAF. He became a member and later the chairman of the National Sports Council and of the All African Games, held in 1987 in Nairobi. In 1989, he took over from Samuel Mbogo as the NOCK chairman and he became a member of the IOC. For ten years, Mukora presided over the National Olympic Committee before he was forced out of the office. It was alleged that he had accepted bribes from the bid committee of the Salt Lake City Winter Olympics. When asked about it, Mukora says, "What is a bribe? If you accept that getting a watch or a gift is a bribe, then all of us were bribed."

The charismatic figure was even a member of the parliament before he decided to quit before going for re-election "because of some very dirty tricks like buying out the voting cards." Now, Charles Mukora has passed his seventies but he is still going strong. And he still has some dreams. He started a project helping the poor people in Southern Sudan and he wants elderly Kenyans to get more involved in sports for keeping fit. His mind is as sharp as ever.

A GERMAN MADE A DIFFERENCE

When Walter Abmayr, a sports diploma teacher from Germany, arrived in Kenya in November 1980 with his wife, Sylvia, athletics was on its knees after the boycotts of the Olympics in 1976 and 1980. There were power struggles going on between the athletics federation and the Ministry for Culture and Social Services, which included the sport.

Abmayr came within the framework of a project for technical assistance in the Third World, financed by the German government for developing the sports of athletics on a large scale. Earlier in his professional career, he had already been in Nigeria, in Southeast Asia, in Ghana, he has also been a German national coach and, since 1977, an IOC Olympic Solidarity lecturer.

W.A. *"When I arrived, the working conditions were not easy. There was a lot of in-fighting going on. When the British handed over the sports administration to the Kenyans, they left behind a quite well-functional sports infrastructure. In all the regions there were a lot of sports facilities which had been used on a regular basis. But after independence the money was not flowing anymore, or rather not used particularly well for developing athletics. Remnants of the colonial period, like Archie Evans and John Velzian, kept the sport going to a certain extent. But the Kenyans, now independent, wanted to run sports on themselves. Both, the British and the Kenyans, Charles Mukora and others, claim to be responsible for the successes between 1956 and 1972. It is difficult to judge, especially when you consider the way Kenyan athletes, as well as coaches and teachers, have always been autodidacts. In the course of the years there was a lot of help and influence coming from different countries and individuals, scholarships in the U.S. and in Europe, etc. In my assignment in Kenya, I had to work as a national coach, an administrator and a lecturer."*

Walter Abmayr's main task, however, was not to train athletes, even though he was working as a national coach and went with the team to the World Cup 1981, the African Championships and the Commonwealth Games 1982, the World Championships 1983, as well as the World Cross-country Championships 1983 and 1985. His number one priority was getting Kenyan athletes back to the top by building up an infrastructure for local competitions and by training athletics coaches at all levels.

During the time Abmayr was in the country, more than 500 Kenyans completed the courses successfully: 336 coaches at the C level, 114 at the B level and 52 at the very taxing A level. A diploma coaching course was the last and final step in this program, which was completely financed by the German government. At the end of Abmayr's time, 42 diploma coaches had come out of the program. Since 1962 the German Foreign Office promoted sports in Third World countries. In 1983-1984 almost $ 1.5 million US had been provided for different countries, mainly for athletics and soccer but also for hockey, swimming, handball and boxing. Even the Nyayo Stadium in Nairobi was built with German support and know-how. It was the first stadium in Kenya with a synthetic track.

Abmayr at the home of Naftali Temu

For years, Abmayr was the personal coach of such people as Juma Ndiwa (800m 1:44.20), James Atuti (400m 44.98), Julius Korir (Olympic gold medallist at the Los Angeles Games 1984 in the steeplechase) and Kipkemboi Kimeli whom he took in at the age of 15. In 1985, Kimeli became the first-ever Kenyan winner at the World Cross-country Championships at Lisbon, in the junior's category. In 1988 in Seoul – at that time Kimeli lived with the Abmayrs in Germany – he won an Olympic bronze in the 10,000m.

Walter Abmayr arranged training camps for the national team at Nyahururu for the cross-country season and at Kiganjo for the track. Kiganjo, a village in the west of Mount Kenya was well known for the police training college where, in the sixties, even Kipchoge Keino came from. The German introduced training programs that were followed in the whole of Kenya. The one for the cross-country season was still being used by Mike Kosgei ten years later. (See the program in Part 3 of this book.)

W.A. *"I really had a great time in Kenya. When I went there my wife was expecting. In 1981, Julia Adhiambo was born, in 1984, Manuela Chebet and in 1986, after our return to Germany, our son Alexander Kemboi. Their names will always remind us of the fantastic time full of life we experienced in Kenya. For the last 25 years I watched all the national cross-country championships, beginning with the one which was held in 1981 at the Kabarak farm of President Daniel arap Moi. I never stopped coaching and later managed some Kenyans when they came to Europe. Several times I and my family came to Kenya for lectures or holidays. And I still have a lot of very good friends there, for example Mike Kosgei who became my successor as the national coach. I was the witness to his marriage and he named his son Walter after me."*

WALTER ABMAYR´S KEY POINTS

- In Kenya, sport has a very high acceptance and reputation. The more successful an athlete is, the more he is accepted. Athletics has a tradition. And, for many young boys and girls, it is still one of the only ways to make money.

- From their childhood, the Kenyans have very good prerequisites for their physical development because most of them grow up in a natural, rural environment where they are used to walking a lot in order to secure their fundamental needs. The simple way of life, the healthy food and the altitude all play a role. The genetics also play a part: Kenyans are slender and light and have a big heel bone that helps pushing the stride.

- African athletes don't have the same stress load as Westerners. They are somehow naïve but, at the same time, they do not have too much respect when confronting top names. They don't know fear and have a lot of self-confidence.

- In the Western world, with its scientific-intellectual way of thinking, we believe that you should run in a steady pace. We trust in measuring the lactate acid, which is supposed to indicate the level of intensity. I am convinced that by doing that we get in a wrong direction. Most of the Western runners cannot cope with changing the pace because they are not used to doing it while training. When Kenyans go for an easy run, all of a sudden one athlete will push the pace and the others take on the challenge and follow. They love playing with the pace. It corresponds with their nature. That is their strength. And they love running in groups.

- In Kenyan society, for a long time, women were not accepted as athletes at all. The woman belongs to the family. She is the one doing most of the hard work in the house and on the farm. Even in the 21st century things change slowly. That is one of the main reasons why there are not more Kenyan female runners. But, there is still a great potential.

THE SLY FOX WHO LED THE NATIONAL TEAM FOR 15 YEARS

Michael "Mike" Kosgei was the national coach for 15 years, from 1985-1995 and from 2001-2004. He was there when John Ngugi won the first individual gold medal for Kenya at the World Cross-Country Championships 1986 in Switzerland; he was there when Ezekiel Kemboi, Brimin Kipruto and Paul Kipsiele Koech went away with all three steeplechase medals at the Olympics 2004 in Athens, the second "clean sweep" for the Kenyan team after the Barcelona Olympics in 1992.

Who is this man who has celebrated more medals in the last two decades than any other coach in the world?

M.K. *"In school I became a star in sprinting and I was taken to St. Patrick's in 1971 after running 10.8 – without shoes! When I left Iten in 1974, I had already changed to the 800 meters. That helped me to get a scholarship in the USA at Washington State University. A few Kenyans were already there. I was not a great runner, but I was running anyway. Once, I ran 1:46, but most of the time it was 1:49, 1:50 – at least good enough to maintain the scholarship. When I was at Washington State, Samson Kimobwa joined and then in 1976 Henry Rono. Henry introduced me to the long distances and in 1978 I was even running a marathon: 2 hours 32 in Oregon. Not bad for somebody who used to be a sprinter."*

Kosgei received his Bachelor's degree in Social Science in 1979 and then went back to Kenya. He worked for the Ministry of Culture and Social Services, which included sports. After a short time, he became executive officer for the

Kenyan Amateur Athletics Federation. In this capacity, he was given the assignment of taking Walter Abmayr around the country to show him places where the athletes were training. Abmayr had come to Kenya for teaching coaches. Within a short time, the German had full trust in the young, determined man and decided to help him in becoming a coach himself. When Abmayr started organizing courses on the different levels, Kosgei was always in the first group, and in 1982, Kosgei traveled as Abmayr's assistant to the Commonwealth Games in Brisbane.

With the help of his mentor, Mike Kosgei got a scholarship for studying sports at Mainz University. He went to Germany for eighteen months. When he came back, it was almost the end of 1984. In March 1985, Abmayr and Kosgei celebrated the first-ever gold at the World Cross-country Championships in Lisbon by the junior, Kipkemboi Kimeli. In the same year, Abmayr's contract expired and Mike Kosgei became the national coach.

With Kosgei, big success came: first with individual and men's team titles in 1986, and two years later in Auckland an amazing performance with four out of six titles and incredible individual positions: 1, 2, 3, 4, 6, 7, 8, 9 in the men's category and 1, 2, 4, 5, 6 in the junior men's. An even more impressive outcome happened in 1993. Kenya went away with all the three medals in the men's race, the junior men and the junior women, as well as all the four team titles – 13 out of 16 medals, and 1994 with seven out of eight gold medals! "Magic Kosgei" had made it possible. Kenya's dominance lasted for 16 years, from 1987 until 2002, but when Ethiopia came up with the magnificent Kenenisa Bekele and some strong female runners, the overall team classification now tipped in favor of the neighbor to the north.

M.K. *"The purpose of cross-country was to prepare the athletes for the track season. My driving force was not the cross-country itself. I wouldn't say our athletes were in superb form when they went to the World Cross, but they had a lot of strength that I was emphasizing by climbing hills and doing the strength work, combined with a little bit of speed, sometimes on the road. I had a good systematic training formula. I don't want to take the whole credit.*

All the coaches were working hard. You cannot come and lead somebody in one month to the top. When the athletes reported at the camp, they all were in good shape, otherwise they could not have made the team. It is like a tea factory. There are many processes. I am the one who knows how to refine the tea, to make it first class. It is the talent God has given me. I have good powers of observation and psychology.

You have to know how to talk to the athletes, when to use authority and when to use democracy, when to be tough and when it is time for socializing with them. The program itself was never magic. My success was the teamwork. There was no championship where we went without a proper tactical plan."

In the eighties and nineties, coaching a Kenyan national team was an easier task than it is today. For one thing, the athletes didn't have mobile phones. That meant the personal coaches could not get in touch with them. The coaches in the camp decided the training program. In the era of modern communications, a personal coach will send an e-mail or an SMS and ask the athlete about the program for the following day. Then the athlete might answer: "They have given us hill work," upon which the coach could say: "Don't do this."

M.K. *"When everybody starts following his own program, in the race say, maybe the strength is not equal. And also you cannot plan tactics because you don't have the indications about the personal strengths and weaknesses. We used to test the athletes in different ways. That is when not only the coach but also the athletes themselves saw who were the strongest in the team, and then they accepted my orders without any problems."*

Annemari Sandell: training and eating with the Kenyans

Is Mike Kosgei one of the best middle and long distance coaches the world has ever seen? Looking at his record with the Kenyan national team or at the fact that he helped lead the Finnish athlete Annemari Sandell to the World Cross-Country junior title 1995 in Durham, one would definitely agree. The coup with Sandell was especially impressive. Sandell had trained in Kenya for six weeks, including three weeks with the national team, three times a day. She became her country's first World Cross-Country Champion since Pekka Päivärinta 22 years earlier. No wonder, Kosgei lost his job with the federation a few months later. He then went to Finland until 1998.

Mike Kosgei

When he came back, he worked briefly for Rosa & Associati and the IAAF/IOC high performance center at Eldoret before he was reinstated as the national coach. But after the Athens' Olympics, Kosgei was fired once more. This time he seems to have burned his bridges. He signed a three-year contract with Spear Sports Management as their coach at Kapsabet, the place where he comes from.

One thing is for sure. When it comes to motivating the athletes or preparing them tactically, you would hardly find a better coach. When he gets the opportunity to talk about it, he turns into a different man. His eyes start shining, and his face shows a mischievous grin. Even after years, he can still laugh about those tricks as if they had happened just yesterday. That is when the serious debater becomes the sly fox.

M.K. *"Let me give you two examples. As we all know, Haile Gebrselassie was the dominant long distance runner in the nineties. But he was beaten in the 5,000 meters at the World Championships in 1993 because he didn't follow Mike Chesire who was leading up to 1,600m after an astonishing first kilometer in 2:31min. And then Ismael Kirui took over and was winning the race despite Gebrselassie's last lap of 56.5. When it came to the World Cross-Country Championships the next year at Budapest, I knew he will not let any Kenyan go without following him. So I set Joseph Kariuki to run only 100 meters. After 50 meters, the announcer said, this is the fastest ever cross-country. And I knew Gebrselassie was going to be*

with this man. Then Wilson Omwoyo took the next six kilometers. Gebre was still with the leading Kenyan. After six kilometers, 'Rambo' Songok came. Gebre was confused. Now, for a short time, Paul Tergat took over and then Simon Chemoiywo.

Kosgei at home with his family

Approaching the final straight, William Sigei, Chemoiywo, Tergat and Gebrselassie were all in a position to win. But by then Gebrselassie was exhausted after following all the leading Kenyans and was outkicked by Sigei and Chemoiywo. It was exactly according to our plan."

"At the World Championships 2003, we had four guys in the 5,000m final, defending champion Richard Limo, Eliud Kipchoge, John Kibowen and Abraham Chebii. I knew our best bet would be Eliud. The day before the race I asked Moses Kiptanui, who was the head coach in Paris, if he had talked to the athletes. He said, no, I cannot talk to them because they have different managers. So I told the boys, let us have early lunch and let us meet at the warm-up track. I wanted to talk to them immediately before they went to the competition so that nobody else could interfere. When I went there, I found them sitting down. They had not started warming up. I said, 'Gentlemen, can you tell me how you are going to run? Have you discussed?' They said, no. I said, 'Okay, you discuss and then you tell me.' I pretended I wanted to walk away. Before I finished two steps, they called me, 'Coach, we don't know. You come and tell us.' So I said, 'Limo you are the one who has to keep the pace high because there is El Guerrouj in the race who has a terrible kick and also Bekele. Limo is to be followed by Eliud.'

And I told Kibowen and Chebii, 'Sit and watch. Whenever you see a mistake you take over. Let the boys do the job.' And then Chebii assisted me, and he said, 'Coach, and what about if the gun goes and Bekele starts pushing?' I said, 'Limo is still to follow. But listen, gentlemen, if he goes, he will lead for three laps hard. And then he will slow down. And he will go again in the fifth lap. And that is when he will leave you behind.

So, as soon as you see him slowing down, you guys take over.' Then I said, 'Eliud, with three laps to go, it is your turn.' He looked concerned and said, 'coach this is too early.' So, I told him, I am not telling you, you have to sprint for three laps. I am telling you be aware like a child is aware of the snake. The fight is going to come from El Guerrouj. Anytime he is going to start moving. Anytime. And he is going to run the last 800 as fast as possible. And he will not slow down. He will finish with his speed. Follow him! With 50 meters to go, you just streak a little bit – he will not wake up anymore!"

Kosgei nearly dies laughing. Once again it worked out. Eliud Kipchoge became the World Champion, El Guerrouj won silver, Bekele bronze. The athletes followed his instructions because they believed in him. He was able to negotiate with the athletes. He always had that certain something. He believes that the strength of the Ethiopians is also founded in the good teamwork between the athletes and the national coach. If a manager has confidence in the coach, he will not interfere. But Kosgei agrees that the federation has to play a more active role, too.

M.K. *"As long as the Kenyans are scattered all over the world, they will not see World Records for some time – unless by luck. So, it is my prayer that the people in the federation will see this. They should start accepting professionalism. So far they pick athletes and coaches a few weeks before a major championship and think this is enough. But it isn't. A personal coach is like a pilot. If the show is in London and you pick anybody instead of the pilot to take the plane there, it can* *be a disaster. I believe that the best athletes have to train together, at least for six months or even for the whole year. From there they can be called by their managers for the races abroad. But of course it can only work if Athletics Kenya is ready to employ several coaches and spend money, even for allowances and compensations. And this might be the main problem – at least as long as we have the present crew in power."*

One indication that the Kenyan athletics federation doesn't like spending money on others can be found when considering Kosgei's salary when he was the national coach. In 1985, he started with 7,000, later the amount was increased to 14,000. In the final years, he earned 29,000 a month, expenses included. Not U.S. dollars, mind you, but Kenya Shillings. 29,000 Ksh are equivalent to $ 390 US!

- I think the main difference between athletes from Europe and the USA and the ones from Kenya is that in the Western world people cannot survive without going to work. In Kenya, most of the athletes have a lot of time. They can train three times a day, maybe six hours altogether. And they are hungry in the real sense of the word. If you train only two or three hours, you will never reach the same level.

- When Europeans or Americans are running together, using stop watches and heart monitors, you can see for them it is a very serious matter, almost like work. Africans start running, mostly slowly, and then they accelerate. For them, it is a kind of a game. You try to challenge the other. If you want to be successful, you have to enjoy your training. When you take it too seriously, it damages your thinking and put you down. But if you go and say, okay, it is a game, man, let's do it, it's fun–then you will not use a lot of mental strength.

- After having a bad workout, a European might think about it for many days. It can really affect him, and he might lose days of good training. A Kenyan will forget about it immediately. If I was not strong today, I will be next time. It started with our great-grandfathers. When they had to look after the cattle, they used to wrestle to pass the time. So when you wrestle and your opponent puts you down, you don't believe he has beaten you. It is only that he took it today. Kenyans have transferred this philosophy to the track. When you break a World Record, they say, okay, tomorrow it is my turn. A European would say, what,

26 minutes and 17 seconds for the World Record at 10,000 meters – forget it. For Africans, the challenge is in their blood, running is in their blood.

- I think all the training programs in this world are more or less equal. It is only the question of dedication and finding the right path to follow.

- People in Europe and the USA have especially rushed too much into science when it comes to nutrition and training. Advertisments tell you, if you eat this, you'll get energy, if you eat that, you'll run faster. But the fact is that people can still break World Records with their natural food. And when it comes to the training, running in the forest is still better than running on a treadmill in the house. The air you breathe outside is better and the environment is a blessing for body and mind.

- Athletes should avoid training on the tarmac and on a synthetic track because it brings a lot of injuries. The shoes are never good enough to train on the tarmac. It has been discovered that a lot of injuries come also from running on synthetic tracks. A murrum track is much better. Make sure you always wear the right clothes. And when it is hot, drink enough. When you lose water, you get injuries. Let us follow the tradition!

FROM A NIGHT CLUB MUSICIAN TO A TOP COACH

If you were spending your vacation in Mombasa during the '70s, you might have paid a visit to a popular night club. The place would have been packed with tourists and sailors from all over the world. Cigarette smoke burns in your eyes until they leave the main door open to get some air. On the stage, there is a band playing music. The percussionist is a man in his '20s. He plays Congo drums, flutes – and a variety of different instruments. Imagine that this man will one day be one of the most successful running coaches. The man who helped Moses Kiptanui and Daniel Komen to the top of world athletics. This is the story of Jimmy "Simba" Beauttah.

J.B. *"After school I did a bit of music all along the coast in the beach hotels in and around Mombasa. I was a percussionist in a dance band. I was the man who puts a different taste to the music. In 1974, we played at the Sunshine night club. It was crowded. I don't know if it was because of the music we played, because of the beer – or because of the ladies. We were to go for an interval when an officer from the Navy came and asked me if he could see me outside. He told me he was given the responsibility of forming a band. He has been frequenting the club for some time and he thought that I could be the one he was looking for. I gave it a thought. I went to my elder brother and asked him how he liked the idea. I asked my sister and my mother. They said, maybe your star could shine in the Armed Forces. I thought, okay, that would give me experience about life because in the forces you have people from different places. And I thought this is a government institution so it might be easy for me to come up with recording my own music and maybe get good instruments. After a few days, I said yes to the officer, even though I knew that I had to sign up for nine years."*

Jimmy Beauttah

The course was set for a career as a Navy musician. Beauttah's band was called "The Pirates Band Kenya Navy." When on stage, they would cover one of their eyes. They played on the shore, in the barracks and on the base. They played music for the Navy, but they also played for civilians. Sometimes they played in the beach hotels, at wedding ceremonies or fundraisers. Jimmy Beauttah did this job for several years. During that period, to keep himself fit and disciplined, he practiced boxing and karate. He says his boxing was "barrack level." He didn't want to go professional because he still needed his hands for his music. As a boxer, Jimmy "Simba" – the lion – became the sparring partner of some of the international boxers in the Navy at that time.

Nevertheless, his music career didn't develop the way he had hoped. There was no chance of recording his own music, and he didn't intend to play just for pleasure but as a professional, to make money. He also wanted to compose music, but it didn't materialize. That was the point when he knew he needed a change.

Laban Rotich at Nyhururu

J.B. *"I think it was in 1978 when I decided to go into sports. I became a physical instructor for keeping people fit, from the commander to the recruits. When you go for these courses as a fitness instructor, you touch a lot of different sports. In the early '80s, I got the opportunity to attend the athletics coaching courses organized by the German, Walter Abmayr and that is when I specialised in athletics. I am glad and give thanks to God for making it possible. Later, I was an instructor for the Armed Forces training college at Lanet near Nakururu. I also worked in the Department of Defence in Nairobi. It was in 1995, after 21 years, when I retired from the Armed Forces"*

In 1991, he met the British agent, Kim McDonald, which changed his life completely. Beauttah was appointed manager and coach for the World Indoor Championships at Seville. After that he worked as Kim McDonald's associate. He was looking after the company's athletes who at that time came mostly from the Armed Forces. After retiring from the Forces, Jimmy Beauttah started the permanent camp at Nyahururu for Kim Management. For some years, they stayed at the

Kawa Falls Hotel before the company rented some residential apartments in town. I remember very well when I first went there. Beauttah's small hotel room was also his living room where he received athletes for individual talks and the place where he massaged and treated the athletes when they had an injury.

The Kawa Falls Hotel

The free weights, the medicine balls and all the other training equipments were stacked up in one corner of the room. Jimmy Beauttah was not only coach, he was at the same time physiotherapist, father, friend and pastor.

J.B. *"I saw some of the athletes when they did the Grand Prix races. Before the season ended, their performances declined because of lack of basic preparation. At Nyahururu, we had all the athletes at one place. We could train these people together and make sure that everybody who was going to Europe was well prepared. It worked out very well. A lot of very good performances had their roots in our camp. I was in charge of the basic training in Kenya, Kim was busy organizing the races. In later years, sometimes Moses Kiptanui would assist me. I used to travel to Europe quite often with the athletes. After the death of Kim in 2001 things went a bit wrong. First, Daniel Komen decided to start his own camp near Kaptagat, and then Moses Kiptanui left Nyahururu and went to Eldoret. There they could also concentrate on their businesses. Kim had always preferred people to stay at Nyahururu. That was the central point. This place didn't belong to Kikuyus or Kalenjins. At Nyahururu, there were athletes from different tribes. To Kim, tribes didn't matter."*

It is said that Moses Kiptanui and Daniel Komen had their differences. Kiptanui was a kind of assistant to Beauttah and at the same time he was a shareholder of Kim's management. But starting in 1996 and 1997, Komen was on everyone's lips and not Kiptanui anymore. Anyway, the Nyahururu camp was still alive. People like the two Tanzanians, John Yuda and Fabian Joseph, used to train there and many others, especially young athletes. Nevertheless, in 2004, Jimmy Beauttah decided to take up a new challenge. He became the coach for the IAAF/IOC high performance training center at Eldoret. One of the athletes who came out of this camp was, Daniel Kipchircir Komen.

In his years at Nyahururu, Jimmy Beauttah included sprinting in the long distance training, and he valued the general fitness and body conditioning for his athletes. He believes that these are the main reasons that so many top athletes were produced in his camp. Now he asks himself why Kenyan athletes are not able to win major championships or to break world records anymore.

J.B. *"I wonder, I wonder. The new generation is also very talented, no doubt about it. I think it is the attitude. They are not patient enough. They see Moses' or Daniel's big cars in town, they see their big houses, and they want the same within a short time. They forget that there is no direct way from the primary school to the college. You have to do your exams before you can go to the next stage. It is the same with an athlete. There is no shortcut. I don't blame the managers, at least not the established ones. Many young athletes are only thinking about quick money and want to run in as many races as possible. It took Moses Kiptanui many years to be able to put up a business center in Eldoret. Maybe Moses and Daniel had an advantage. They had a peaceful time to prepare and climb step by step because no one before them went up to that level."*

Nyahururu's landmark: the Thompson Falls

"When we talk about the national team, there is only one way: incentives. A long time ago the IAAF meant International Amateur Athletics Federation, now it is the International Association of Athletics Federations. The 'Amateur' is gone. Even the Kenyan federation changed its name from Kenyan Amateur Athletics Association to Athletics Kenya. When we talk about championships, remember in the past a winner got a gold medal – and only glory. Nowadays, you go home with the medal and $ 60,000 US. The teammates will not sacrifice their chances as long as they don't get a share. Athletics is a professional sport. Therefore, the government and the federation have to come up with a proposal on how to compensate the athletes. The other thing: Now the best athletes go directly to the trials where there are only finals. National championships and trials should be together so that the athletes get used to going through heats and semis. And it should not be allowed to have pacemakers. The new athletes especially need to get this feeling of championships. In the Grand Prix events, you follow the pacemaker, but in a championship it depends on you and your thinking ability. What is also very important is the communication between the national coach and the personal coaches. This communication doesn't exist. The best thing they do in the offices of Athletics Kenya is prepare the calendar of the events."

JIMMY BEAUTTAH´S KEY POINTS

- A good coach is somebody who looks after the athlete before himself. It is like a relationship between a father and his child. Behind every succesful man there is a woman, and behind every successful athlete, there is a coach. As an athlete, you don't see the way you are running. You need a third eye. This third eye is the coach. I am there to work on the athlete's weakness day by day. I see the weakness, and I look for something that will correct it. Let the glory be to the athlete and to God.

- Before the athletes go to sleep, I want them to know what tomorrow's training will be. After the session, I explain to them why we did our acivities. When an athlete comes to the camp, he is hungry to get a different recipe. He is ready to learn and accept. What you need to do as the coach is create a friendly atmosphere. You can be firm but friendly. We don't discuss the training sessions every day, but at the end of the week, we sit together and talk.

- Even if I have 30 athletes in my group, it is still possible to coach them individually. There are three different groups. In the A group we have the athletes who are ready for races, then we have the B group with the ones who still need some adjustments. The athletes in the C group are still far behind. After some time, an athlete can be promoted or relegated. When you go to a competition that is where you can see what is lacking. And then you give different workouts.

- When it comes to mileage, fartleks or track workouts, there is not a big difference from one coach to another. I was always using some specialities. Sometimes we would go for a run, let's say one and a quarter hour. Straight from the run, when the athletes have that state of fatigue in the muscles, is when we start sprinting, maybe 10 times 100 meters. This can be once a week. The other thing we did maybe once a week: Speed steps or sprinting with a tire, which is fixed on a rope and a belt around your waist. Pulling that tire develops some extra ability in the muscle structure. When he is without the tire, his legs are stronger. I also used elastic bands and sometimes free weights and medicine balls to condition the body. All these elements are used individually according to the athlete's fitness level. Early in the year, the repetitions may be many and slow, later short and fast. Even Moses Kiptanui and Daniel Komen used to run with the tire.

- A distance runner, or at least his coach, should be aware of how important an efficient movement is. Distance runners have to be anxious to save energy and to avoid wasteful movements – to get speed with the minimum outlay of energy.

BEAUTTAH'S MOST SUCCESSFUL ATHLETES

Moses Kiptanui:	World Champion at 3,000m steeplechase in 1991, 1993 and 1995, 2nd Olympic Games at 3,000m st in 1996, World Junior Champion at 1,500m in 1990. World Records at 3,000m in 1992 (7:28.96), 5,000m in 1995 (12:55.30), 3,000m st in 1992 (8:02.08) and 1995 (7:59.18), World Indoor Records at 3,000m in 1992 (7:37.31) and 1995 (7:35.13)
William Tanui:	Olympic Champion at 800m in 1992, 3rd World Indoor Championships at 1,500m in 1997
Paul Rutto:	World Champion at 800m in 1993
Paul Bitok:	2nd Olympic Games at 5,000m in 1992 and 1996, 2nd World Indoor Championships at 3,000m in 1997 and 1999
Joseph Keter:	Olympic Champion at 3,000m steeplechase in 1996
Daniel Komen:	World Champion at 5,000m in 1997, World Junior Champion at 5,000m and 10,000m in 1994. World Records

at 3,000m in 1996 (7:20.67), 5,000m in 1997 (12:39.74), 2 miles in 1996 (8:03.54) and 1997 (7:58.61), World Indoor Records at 3,000m in 1998 (7:24.90) and 5,000m in 1998 (12:51.48), World Junior Records at 1,500m and 5,000m in 1995

Paul Koech: World Half-marathon Champion in 1998, 2nd World Cross-Country Championships in 1998. World Road Best at 10 miles in 1997 (44:45)

John Kibowen: World Cross-country Champion at 4km in 1998 and 2000, 2nd in 2003, 3rd World Championships at 5,000m in 2001

Noah Ngeny: Olympic Champion at 1,500m in 2000, 2nd World Championships at 1,500m in 1999, 3rd World Indoor Championships at 1,500m in 2001. World Record at 1,000m in 1999 (2:11.96)

Sammy Kipketer: Commonwealth Champion at 5,000m in 2002, 2nd World Cross-Country Championships at 4km in 2000. World Junior Record at 3,000m in 1999 (7:34.58), World Road Best at 5km in 2000 and 2001 (13:00) and 10km in 2001 and 2002 (27:11)

Benjamin Limo: World Champion at 5,000m in 2005, 2nd in 1999, World Cross-Country Champion at 4km in 1999, 3rd in 2001 and 2003, 2nd Commonwealth Games at 5,000m in 2002

Abraham Chebii: 2nd World Cross-Country Championships at 4km in 2005

John Yuda (Tan): 3rd World Half-Marathon Championships in 2001 and 2002, 2nd World Cross-Country Championships in 2002

Fabian Joseph (Tan): World Half-Marathon Champion in 2005, 2nd in 2002 and 2004

Others include Joseph Tengelei, Vincent Malakwen, Ondoro Osoro, Laban Rotich, Tom Nyariki, David Kiptoo, Patrick Ndururi, Luke Kipkosgei, John Kosgei, Martin Keino, Shadrack Korir, Joseph Riri, Jackline Maranga.

THE IRISH BROTHER
WHOSE ATHLETES BECAME
WORLD-BEATERS

His story is like a fairytale. When Colm O'Connell, a 28-year-old Irish Patrician Brother from Cork, decided to take on a teaching job in the small Kenyan town of Iten, he never expected that he would become the country's most successful middle distance coach of all time. Brother Colm had neither been an athlete nor a coach before. He came as an ordinary teacher, but such is life.

B.C. *"Before I came, I knew St Patrick's had a reputation for athletics. Mike Boit had passed through and left the school in 1969. When I arrived in 1976, I was plunged into a sporting arena. There was a whole sports program in place. Peter Foster, the brother of the well-known British athlete, Brendan, was there as one of the athletic coaches. I obviously got involved in the sports programs myself. Remember at that time Iten was a very rural area. There was no tarmac road, no electricity, no telephone service and no reliable running water system. Of course, it was a big difference to the life I was used to in Ireland. On the other hand: hardship was part of our way of life in Ireland in the fifties. That time in Kenya you lived a very isolated life in the sense that here you were in a small rural village and you had to find ways of occupying yourself. I used sport also as a way of integrating myself. I remember very well when Peter Foster came to me one day and said, "why don't you think of doing some athletics?" My first thought was what do I know about athletics? I mean, back in Ireland I watched on TV as Kipchoge Keino won his gold medals at the Olympics, and I knew Kenyans were good in running. But I knew absolutely nothing about coaching an athlete. And I had never been to an athletics competition in my whole life."*

Peter Foster was the one who encouraged Brother Colm by telling him, "You will learn about it. Here in Kenya is the best place to learn. There are talented people. You just come along the track. You watch how they train. You talk to them. You see competitions. The technicality will come. Start with the interest. You can develop the know-how."

Brother Colm acknowledges that at the beginning there was a certain element of trial and error. Because St Patrick's is a boarding school, the kids were there 24 hours, seven days a week. They were always at the teacher's disposal. When they came out of class, they were there. So what do you do? You organize a competition. There was not much more entertainment going on other than sports. No videos, no mobile phones, no computer games, no burger restaurants.

B.C. *"I kind of became associated with athletics, so to speak. The kids now saw you as an athletics coach. They saw you as somebody who has an interest in sport. That put a little bit of a challenge on me to learn more about the sport and to become more focused as to who the athletes are and about their strengths and weaknesses. Gradually, I started to learn. Maybe at the beginning you could call me a kind of a social coach in the sense that I was only for interaction, being with them in competitions, but not the one who decided about the daily programs. We didn't even have a real program at that time. Every day we discussed and decided what we would do."*

At the end of 1979-80, after Peter Foster had left, Colm O'Connell became responsible for athletics in the school. That meant training the athletes every day, going to the competitions with them and making sure they had the training equipment they needed. At that time, there were some outstanding schools for athletics in the country with very strong teams. There used to be various inter-school-competitions before the actual overall school championships began.

St. Patrick's High School

In the early '80s, Brother Colm completed coaching courses under Walter Abmayr. He was with Jimmy Beauttah and Mike Kosgei in the first group of coaches. Now, for the first time, he could really say that he identified and developed athletes, people like the Cheruiyot twins and Peter Rono who became the 1500 meters Olympic Champion in 1988 in Seoul.

At that time, many athletes went to the United States. The only outlets for good athletes coming out of secondary school in Kenya were the Armed Forces, the Police, the Prison Service and Kecoso (Kenya Communications Sports Organization). Kecoso hired a lot of people, and since they lost their interest, Kenya didn't produce top athletes in the sprinting and field events anymore. Kenya Railways had a team, Kenya Ports Authority had a team, Telkom Kenya had a team, and they all had athletes in the different events.

So even high jumpers or shot putters got a job in one of these companies. If the athlete didn't like these options, there was one more: America.

The different camps, organized and financed by European managers, started only in the early '90s.

B.C. *"When the pros came in, all events below 800 meters were cut off – because there was no interest and no money. There was a time Kenyan sprinters won Commonwealth medals. Of course, most sprinters come from West Africa but this doesn't mean there are no sprinters in Kenya – or no athletes for field events. It lacks interest, investment and development. Everybody dived into the pros. And every coach now says: give up the 400 meters, move to 800. In 1985, our school's relay team 4 x 400 meters was second to the army in the national senior championships. They ran 3:06 minutes. This is still our school record. The sprint records still stand since that time. The Kenyan national record for 110 meter hurdles is from the '70s. Do you mean that our present athletes don't have the same genes? The day might come when we will have an absolute breakdown with too many Kenyans in middle and long distance running and road races. The money will drop. Why are so many athletes leaving track events? Why do we have only few doing track today? Because they take 30 Kenyans in a road race but maybe only three in a track event."*

In 1989, Brother Colm moved in a new direction and decided to promote young female athletes as well. He established his first training camp during school holidays.
The first two camps were girls only. Susan Chepkemei, Lydia Cheromei, Lenah Chesire and Caroline Kwambai came out of these programs, and a little bit later Sally Barsosio and Rose Cheruiyot. In the meantime, these camps are held every year

in April for preparing the track season and in December for cross-country and they are open for all the best athletes from the Rift Valley Province. He is working with five other coaches. They have a fairly wide area where they identify young talents in the age group of 15 or 16 years, boys and girls. They follow the athletes for a season or two before they invite them to the camp. Even when they bring them to the training camp, the first year or two is getting to know them and the kids getting to know the specific training sessions and their purpose. (See training programs in the chapter "How they trained in the early days and how they train now.")

It was in the mid-nineties when O'Connell started coaching professional athletes, people like Japhet Kimutai who broke the World Junior Record at 800m in 1998 and Kipkurui Misoi, in the late '90s one of the best steeplechasers in the world. Coaching people who had decided to put all their efforts into an athletics career was a big challenge and responsibility for the Irishman. He had to start thinking on a new level. Now he started following the sport in Europe, going occasionally to competitions and talking to different coaches.

B.C. *"Zurich 1995 was the first time I ever saw a European meet. It was Wilson Kipketer who invited me after winning the world title in Gothenburg. Before, I could not even watch on TV. There was no channel in Kenya that was showing the Grand Prix meets. In Zurich, I saw two World Records by Moses Kiptanui who broke the 8-minute barrier in the steeplechase and by Haile Gebrselassie in the 5,000 meters.*

Brother Colm and Agnes Wamakonjio, in the early nineties the head mistress of the Singore Girls School

In 1996, I went to Brussels and again there were two World Records by Salah Hissou in the 10,000 meters and Svetlana Masterkova in the 1,000. I was a kind of a nobody in the coaching world. At that time the book "Running Free," written by Sebastian Coe and David Miller, gave me quite a lot of input. I realized that Kenyan middle distance runners sometimes don't do enough mileage. They tend to concentrate too much on speed work. Coe did a lot of long runs before the season and the actual specific training of the season. I learned also the importance of exercises. In recent years, I learned more about the importance of gymnasium."

Benson Koech,
World Junior
Champion at
800m in 1992

After Japhet Kimutai there were the Chirchir brothers William and Cornelius and then came Isaac Songok and Augustine Choge. Although Colm O'Connell was now a very experienced coach, especially when it comes to 800 and 1,500 meters, he now had to transform himself into a long distance coach. He did it in a masterly manner. Choge, then only 17 years old, ran the 5,000 meters in 2004 under 13 minutes, and Songok won the Kenyan title in his first year as a 5,000 meter runner in 2005 in a most impressive style but at the World Championships in Helsinki he was not able to cope with the slow, tactical race.

The modest Irishman has brought up more world-class middle distance runners than anybody else. However, he doesn't get any share of the money his athletes and their agents make all over the world. Maybe it is because of his faith in God he accepts the facts without any lament.

B.C. *"I don't look at it like that. If you would always think about who is going to reward you before you do something in this life, you would not do anything. Some athletes they appreciate what you did for them and they will come back and organize maybe some equipment but others they don't. For eight or ten years, I worked very closely with the British agent Kim McDonald. He was very supportive for our program. The great thing was even though he invested a lot of money in our camps, he knew that it didn't guarantee him to get all the best athletes. After Kim passed away, we were struggling for a little while and sometimes I had to add my personal support.*

We reduced the size of the camp from about 80 to 100 athletes to 50 or 60. In the future, I hope I can leave more to the five coaches I am working with, so that I can concentrate more on my top athletes. I strongly believe that top-class athletes need to have their individual coaches. Over the years, the whole sport became more professional, and only the athletes who are surrounded by a professional team, including a coach, a physiotherapist and a doctor, will be able to stay at the top. Even in a country like Kenya."

BROTHER COLM´S KEY POINTS

- I am not interested in other coaches' programs as such because you have to develop a program with an athlete. It is not imposed on the athlete.

- In October, after a month or two's rest, I sit down with my athletes. First of all, we do a post-mortem. We look at the successes and failures of the season just finished. I let the athlete do a lot of the analysis. What races did you run best and why? The next couple of weeks we spend looking forward. Now we plan based on what we know. That is now when the agent comes in.

- The way I coach: I build an athlete up to a certain level. And I consolidate on that level until I am sure that any time he goes out to run a race this will be his minimum performance. Then I push him to the next level. My coaching is step by step, like climbing stairs.

- Many athletes, when they lose a race, they go back home and start doing an excessive amount of speed work for the next two weeks or so. Speedwork is okay and it is great to have speed in your legs. But in order to be effective in a race you have to be up with the leaders. So you must make sure that the speed is combined with the endurance to be with the leader.

- To develop the leg speed and leg turnover, I use a lot of exercises, a lot of striding patterns and work in the gymnasium. And that must be done in the early season. That speed must be built up through strength, core strength and muscle development in the thighs.

- Everywhere there are athletes who are talented. But talent itself is not enough. I prefer a little bit less talent and a little bit more of the supportive aspects of training, like personality, education and mental toughness. I think in today's world of athletics an athlete has to be more than just a runner. He or she has to have ability to handle the programs, ability to deal with managers, agencies, meet promoters, the press and deal with being a role model to be successful in the sport.

- As a coach, I have to look also at the background of an athlete: the family, the friends and the people who are important in their lives. We have to look at who is influencing the athlete. We have to coordinate that support system.

BROTHER COLM'S MOST SUCCESSFUL ATHLETES

Kipkoech Cheruiyot:	World Junior Record at 1,500m in 1983 (3:34.92)
Charles Cheruiyot:	World Junior Record at 5,000m in 1983 (13:25.33)
Peter Rono:	Olympic Champion at 1,500m in 1988, 2nd World Junior Championships at 1,500m in 1986
Lydia Cheromei:	3rd World Junior Championships at 10,000m in 1990, World Cross-Country Champion Juniors in 1991 (at 13 years!), 3rd 1992, 3rd Women 2001, 2nd World Half-Marathon Championships in 2004. World Junior Record at 5,000m in 1995 (14:53.44)

Matthew Birir:	Olympic Champion at 3,000m steeplechase in 1992, 2nd World Junior Championships at 3,000m st in 1986. World Junior Records at 3,000m st. in 1990 and 1991 (8:24.47)
Benson Koech:	World Junior Champion at 800m in 1992, in 1994 the fastest 800m runner in the world (1:43.17)
Rose Cheruiyot:	2nd World Cross-Country Championships Juniors in 1994, 3rd Women in 1996. World Junior Record at 5,000m in 1995 (14:57.79)
Wilson Kipketer:	World Champion at 800m in 1995, 1997 and 1999, 2nd Olympic Games at 800m in 2000, World Indoor Champion at 800m in 1997. World Record at 800m in 1997 (1:41.11), World Indoor Records at 800m in 1997 (1:42.67) and 1,000m in 2000 (2:14.96); all as a Danish citizen
Sally Barsosio:	World Champion at 10,000m in 1997, 3rd in 1993, 3rd World Junior Championships at 10,000m in 1992, World Cross-country Champion Juniors in 1994, 3rd in 1993, 3rd Women in 1995
Wilson Boit Kipketer:	World Champion at 3,000m steeplechase in 1997, 2nd in 1999, 2nd Olympic Games at 3,000m st. in 2000. World Record at 3,000m st. in 1997 (7:59.08)

Japhet Kimutai:	Commonwealth Champion at 800m in 1998, 2nd World Junior Championships at 800m in 1994. World Junior Record at 800m in 1997 (1:43.64)
Kipkirui Misoi:	3rd Commonwealth Games at 3,000m steeplechase in 1998, 2nd World Junior Championships at 3,000m st. in 1996. World Junior Record at 3,000m st. in 1997 (8:16.76)
William Chirchir:	2nd Commonwealth Games at 1,500m in 2002, World Junior Champion at 800m in 1998. World Junior Record at 1,500m in 1998 (3:33.24)
Cornelius Chirchir:	World Junior Champion at 1,500m in 2000, World Youth Champion at 1,500m in 1999. World Junior Record at 1,500m in 2002 (3:30.24)
Viola Kibiwot:	World Cross-country Champion Juniors in 2002, 3rd in 2000, World Junior Champion at 1,500m in 2002
Isaac Songok:	World Youth Champion at 1,500m in 2001, 3rd World Cross-Country Championships at 4k in 2005, Kenyan national champion at 5,000 m in 2005
Augustine Choge:	World Youth Champion at 3,000m in 2003, World Junior Champion at 5,000m in 2004, World Cross-Country Champion Juniors in 2005. World Youth Record at 5,000m in 2004 (12:57.01) and World Junior Record at 3,000m in 2005 (7:28.78)

A VET IS LOOKING AFTER ELIUD KIPCHOGE AND COMPANY

He is a veterinarian who normally looks after the livestock in his home area. But every day before he treats the sick animals, he takes care of some world-class athletes. Joseph Chelimo is the coach of Eliud Kipchoge, Richard Limo and Brimin Kipruto. He works for Jos Hermens' management company, Global Sports Communication. Their camp is near Kaptagat forest, where the air is full of oxygen, half an hour's drive from Eldoret at an altitude of about 2,300m above sea level. Chelimo works with Patrick Sang who is a former world-class athlete. Sang won three steeplechase silver medals at the Olympics and World Championships in 1991, 1992 and 1993, and he is the coordinator and administrator. Chelimo is in charge of the daily training.

Joseph Chelimo (on the right) with Patrick Sang

J.C. *"Patrick and I, we always discuss the training programs together. We usually have a basic plan for half a year, first for the cross-country season and then for the track season. He is the man responsible for the camp administration, me for the training. But we always help each other. It is a joint venture. I can say, we are a very good, harmonious team."*

How come a vet is dealing with athletes? It all started in 1985. Chelimo came back from a veterinary job in the Central Province and started working in his home area near Kaptagat. That is when he met his former school mate, Joseph Chesire, who at that time was one of the best 1,500 meter runners in the world. When Chelimo heard about Chesire's life as an international runner, he became interested in athletics. After a while the national athletics federation called for elections, Chelimo participated and won a seat in the North Rift federation, and that was the beginning. Then Chelimo wanted to become a coach – and he succeeded within a short time. He was accepted for an IAAF course in Nairobi and passed his exams. Soon after that he finished a second course in which he was acquainted with the rules of track and field.

With the help and introduction by Joseph Chesire, Chelimo was employed by "Dottore" Gabriele Rosa as a coach for his long distance runners. In those days, they used to stay at the Kaptagat Hotel, but before the cooperation had started to become successful and after only six months the liaison was off. Nevertheless, Chelimo now enjoyed his new hobby so much that he decided to coach some athletes from the villages on his own. Sometimes up to one hundred people joined his group. One day, in 1997, Patrick Sang came to see the training. He was impressed, and he asked Chelimo if he would like to work with him. A little bit later the Kenyan tandem was put on the payroll of Global Sports. Since then, they have produced many world-class athletes.

Global Sports now has very nice buildings near Kaptagat where the athletes live when they are preparing for the season.

J.C. *"After they finish the track season, they have a break, one month without doing anything and then a few weeks with a little jogging. November is when the training for the cross-country season starts. We use cross-country as a build-up for the track season. The main components are long runs and speed endurance. The 5000m runners would cover every day at least 25 kilometers. Let's say 1 hour 10 in the morning and between 40 and 50 minutes in the evening. Every Saturday* *they have a long run between 1 hour 30 and 1 hour 40. Speed endurance is what we train with the fartleks, fast for five or six minutes. On Fridays they usually go for hill-work. This can be continuous hill running or hill repetitions."*

"In January we start with more speed work: fartleks with shorter but faster loads. Track workouts usually start after the cross-country season when we prepare for the track. Now we have two, sometimes even three track sessions a week. When we are close to the competitions there are only two, or sometimes three. They still go for long runs during the track season. These long runs are very easy. I strongly believe that it is very important to maintain the endurance level. If you look at my results, I think our program is not too bad."

Chelimo says that over the entire year the training is pretty much the same but what changes is the speed and the number of hard workouts. When they start with track sessions in

Early morning training with the two Swiss Röthlin and Belz

March, they might start with 3 minutes for 1,000 meters, later 2 minutes 50 and then 2 minutes 40. As a rule, the total load is supposed to be slightly more than the distance the athlete is preparing for. For a 5,000-meter runner it means between four and six 1000s. The first races in the season are always at shorter distances: a 5,000m runner might go for a 1,500m and a 3,000m race before he runs his first 5,000m race. The last three or four weeks before a big championship race they ease down the training but incorporate more speed, e.g., 12 x 400m in 60 or 61 seconds with 1 minute recovery, and the long runs might be 1 hour at 60% effort.

- My athletes usually have eleven training sessions a week. From Monday to Friday, two trainings a day and on Saturday the long run. There is no training on Sundays. The only additional sessions they could have are exercises for stability and flexibility. Three sessions a day – this comes mainly from teachers, from coaches who are in schools. Maybe it is because they deal with kids, they prefer to split the daily load into three sessions. My experience tells me that two sessions a day are enough.

- When Europeans come to Kenya and train with Kenyans, they usually come with their own program. Now they try to follow their program and at the same time do some workouts with the Kenyans. Then they end up having a mixed bag. Another aspect: In Europe, many top-class athletes have their own coach who tries to plan all the details. In Kenya, there is one coach for maybe 20 athletes. That means the individual athlete cannot get the same care.

- My athletes get a program where they see, for example, when we go for a track workout but as to what kind of track training we are going to do, I only tell them when we are in the stadium. An athlete has to be ready to take on whatever comes. It makes him mentally strong. And that is why our athletes can cope with any situation in a race. Many Europeans have to know their training program at least one week in advance. When it comes to a competition they need to know all the opponents. And when a new face turns up, they are lost.

- Kenyans take it day by day. That is the way they grew up. Life in our country is tough. This mental strength helps you a lot when it comes to sport. I am convienced it has also to do with the genes. It is a natural selection which started thousand of years ago when only the strongest were able to survive. In Kenya we have 20 athletes who can run the marathon below 2 hours 7 minutes, in the Western world there is one or two.

Joseph
Chelimo

GLOBAL SPORTS' MOST SUCCESSFUL ATHLETES

Bernard Barmasai: 3rd World Championships at 3,000m steeplechase in 1997 and 2001. Commonwealth Games Champion at 3,000m st. in 1998. World Record at 3,000m st. in 1997 (7:55.72)

Reuben Kosgei: Olympic Champion at 3,000m steeplechase in 2000, World Champion at 3,000m st. in 2001, World Junior Champion at 3,000m st. in 1998

Richard Limo: World Champion at 5,000m in 2001, 3rd Commonwealth Games at 5,000m in 1998, 2nd World Cross-Country Championships Juniors in 1998 and 1999. World Junior Record at 3,000m in 1998 (7:34.32)

Michael Kipyego: World Junior Champion at 3,000m steeplechase in 2002

Eliud Kipchoge: World Champion at 5,000m in 2003, 3rd Olympic Games at 5,000m in 2004, World Cross-country Champion Juniors in 2003. World Junior Record at 5,000m in 2003 (12:52.61)

Felix Limo: Winner Rotterdam Marathon in 2004 (2:06:16), Berlin Marathon in 2004 (2:06:44) and Chicago Marathon in 2005 (2:07:02). World Road Best at 15km in 2001 (41:29)

Brimin Kipruto: 2nd Olympic Games at 3,000m steeplechase in 2004, 3rd World Championships at 3,000m st. in 2005, 3rd World Junior Championships at 3,000m st. in 2004, World Youth Champion at 2,000m st. in 2001

Robert Cheboror: Winner Amsterdam Marathon in 2004 (2:06:23)

William Kipsang: Winner Seoul Marathon in 2005

AN ITALIAN TAUGHT KENYANS HOW TO RUN A MARATHON

Before "Dottore" Gabriele Rosa started to coach runners in the East African country, the Kenyan marathon runners hardly existed. In 1990, there was only one Kenyan, Douglas Wakiihuri, among the 20 fastest runners of the year, the next two, Ibrahim Hussein and Daniel Nzokia, between position 80 and 100. But only Nzokia was a "real Kenyan," Wakiihuri lived in Japan, Hussein in the USA. 15 years later you will find that in the top 100, every other is a Kenyan.

It was "Doctor", as he is called respectfully, who transformed Kenya into the leading country of marathon runners.

G.R. *"Marathon didn't have a tradition. All the athletes liked to run cross-country. Even Paul Tergat preferred it. For decades, there were good Kenyan coaches when it came to cross-country. For the track, they were mediocre, but they didn't know much about marathon training. They thought a marathon runner has to run three or four hours in a slow pace. I came and changed the training completely to include more quality, individuality and purpose."*

Gabriele Rosa with Erick Kimayio, manager of the Kapsait camp

When the Italian physician, who was introduced by Moses Tanui, at that time one of the best long distance runners in the world, started working with Kenyan athletes in 1992, he could already call on 20 years experience. As a student, he was coaching his first athletes and later he took over the coaching of some marathon runners of his home area in the neighborhood of the Italian town Brescia. His breakthrough came when Gianni Poli won the prestigious New York City Marathon in 1986. It was, in fact, the third consecutive Italian victory after Orlando Pizzolato's two successes. The two athletes came from two different marathon schools in Italy. Professor Francesco Conconi worked at Ferrara with coach Pier-Paolo Lenzi. Conconi became famous because of the test named after him for defining the anaerobic threshold but also infamous for using blood doping and later EPO.

Rosa has always kept his distance from people like Conconi and his disciple Michele Ferrari and has never worked for the Italian athletics federation (FIDAL) or the national Olympic committee, which that time was experimenting with different performance boosting practices in all the different endurance sports. Gabriele Rosa comes from an aristocratic family. He bears the name of his great-grandfather who was one of the heroes of the Risorgimento, the Italian unification movement in the 19th century. His house looks like an art gallery.

Money has never been Rosa's motivator, but it's the passion and the love for athletics, especially the long distance running. "When I visit an athlete at his home, and I see that in the meantime he was building a new house, it shows me that we are changing many lives, and that makes me happy," he admits. Paul Tergat, Rosa's most successful athlete, says about him: "When Doctor Rosa started coaching me in 1992, I entered a new world. All of a sudden, we did a lot of speed work and speed endurance on the track, something I had never done before. I know him as a very likeable and honest person whose world is running."

In the '90s, "Dottore" Rosa started renting and even building houses at different places in the country where he put up his training camps. There, his athletes were trained by local coaches, all following the programs of the "maestro." For many years, the Italian sport manufacturer Fila was Rosa's main sponsor. They say that the Italian company invested at least $ 1 million US every year for the project in Kenya. There was a time when "Rosa & Associati" had signed up almost 250 Kenyan athletes. But in 2003, when Fila was bought by an American consortium, things changed rapidly. In January 2004, the latest camp at Kapsait in the Cherangani Hills at 3,000 meters above sea level was still officially funded by representatives of Fila USA, but one year later there was a reopening under the flag of Nike. For Gabriele Rosa and his son, Federico, who is taking over his father's legacy slowly but surely, harder times have come. The U.S. giant Nike is not very interested in the work at the grassroots level but more in the top athletes like Paul Tergat, Sammy Korir, Martin Lel and Margaret Okayo. The money is not flowing anymore the way it did in the past. That's why Rosa's company had to drastically reduce the number of athletes. But the distinguished Italian with white hair and white beard who is now in his mid-60s will always be remembered as the one who taught Kenyans how to run a marathon.

Moses Tanui

GABRIELE ROSA´S KEY POINTS

- It is pointless for somebody to go for a three-week training at high altitude only once a year. High-altitude training makes sense only if you stay there for a longer period or several times a year for some weeks.

- There is no doubt that endurance athletes, such as long distance runners, can benefit from the high altitude where you increase the red blood cells that are vital for oxygen transport. Many world-class athletes decided to stay at places like Boulder, Colorado or Flagstaff, Arizona where the altitude is equivalent with the Kenyan highlands. The body adapts after some time to the new conditions, meaning it has more hemoglobin at its disposal and therefore a better oxygen uptake.

- I believe that running in a hilly area is very important for marathon runners. Somebody who always runs on the flat will, after some time, lose his strength. The other point is the mileage. For me, the quality is always much more important than the quantity. I think even top marathon runners don't need to run more than 240 kilometers a week but they have to go on a regular basis for long runs over 30, 35 and even 38 kilometers. For our runners, these long runs are never slow.

- Our marathon training takes three months. The intensity of the training rises more and more every week until the last two weeks when the workload is reduced drastically. For more details, go to Tergat's marathon program in Part 3.

- Some coaches believe in a one-hour runs at a 4-minute per kilometer pace. I don't. My top athletes start maybe at 4'20'' per kilometer and end the session at 3'20'' or 3'10''. "Progressive Running" is what we call it.

- Probably the most important advice for a long distance runner who wants to move up to the marathon: Be patient, it takes years. When you run the 10,000m, your body is consuming a lot of four-star fuel. In the marathon, a completely different biochemistry takes place. You have to use your glycogen economically and burn fat, too. Your body will learn how to burn fat only after a lot of long runs. Apart from this fact, even the running technique is different compared with running on the track where you land much more on the forefoot.

ROSA'S MOST SUCCESSFUL ATHLETES:

Moses Tanui: World Champion at 10,000m in 1991, World Half-marathon Champion in 1995, winner Boston Marathon in 1996 and 1998. World Record at Half-marathon in 1993 (59:47)

Elijah Lagat: Winner Jerez Marathon in 1994, Berlin Marathon in 1997, Prague Marathon in 1998, Boston Marathon in 2000

Paul Tergat: Five-time World Cross-Country Champion (1995-1999), World Half-marathon Champion in 1999 and 2000, winner New York Marathon in 2005. 2nd Olympic Games at 10,000m in 1996 and 2000, 2nd World Championships at 10,000m in 1997 and 1999, 3rd in 1995. World Records at 10,000m in 1997 (26:27.85), Half-marathon in 1998 (59:17) and Marathon in 2003 (2:04:55 in Berlin)

Joseph Chebet: Winner Amsterdam Marathon in 1996, Turin Marathon in 1997, Boston and New York Marathon in 1999

Sammy Korir: Winner Florence Marathon and Cancun Marathon in 1996, Amsterdam Marathon in 1997 and 1999, Turin Marathon in 1999, Beppu Marathon and San Diego Marathon in 2002, 2nd to Tergat in Berlin 2003 (2:04:56)

Alice Timbilil:	World Youth Champion at 3,000m in 1999, 2nd World Cross-country Championships Juniors in 2000, 2nd Women 8km in 2005
Margaret Okayo:	Winner Marathon San Diego in 2000 and 2001, New York 2001 and 2003, Boston 2002, Milan 2002 and London 2004
Charles Kamathi:	World Champion at 10,000m in 2001
Raymond Kipkoech:	Winner Enschede Marathon and Berlin Marathon in 2002, winner Xiamen Marathon in 2005
Robert Cheruiyot:	Winner Boston Marathon in 2003
Martin Lel:	World Half-marathon Champion in 2003. Winner New York Marathon in 2003 and London 2005
Raymond Kipkoech:	Winner Enschede Marathon and Berlin Marathon in 2002, winner Xiamen Marathon in 2005

*"Dottore" Rosa
at the official
opening of the
Kapsait camp in
traditional
outfit*

*Keino lightens the fire
at the Olympic trials
1996 in Nairobi*

PART 3: HOW THEY TRAINED IN THE EARLY DAYS AND HOW THEY TRAIN NOW

KIPCHOGE KEINO: HUGE SUCCESS WITH LITTLE TRAINING

Hezekiah Kipchoge Keino was the first great Kenyan distance runner and, to many, still is the greatest. His achievements were amazing, especially considering the little training he undertook.

Kip Keino grew up in the highlands of the Nandi District. The Nandi Hills have a view unlike anything on Earth. The climate is cool with enough rain for the famous tea plantations and ideal for grazing the cattle. From his younger days, running and jumping was a way of life while he looked after his family's animals.

It was not an easy living for his father, Arap Kurgat. He had to work hard to pay the school fees, buy the uniform and the books. Keino, however, also remembered his mother, who died when he was four years old. She would have been very proud of her son going to school.

The school was not far from home. He used to walk there, but in school, running was a part of the curriculum. He recalls the early days: "I was good in my school but when we went to compete with other schools, I was not even the best – third, fourth, something like that. We were running 800 meters and 400 meters and relays. I used to be in the 4 x 100m and 4 x 400m relay. For us, it was fun. It was only later when I went up to the District and Provincial level that I began to take it seriously."

When he left school, he joined the Police Training College at Kiganjo next to Nyeri, with the eternal snows of Mount Kenya just 50 kilometers away. It was not because of his ambitions as a runner, but because he wanted a job that he knew the police would offer good opportunities. In 1962, when he went back to the college for a promotion, he started to train regularly. In his first year, he qualified for the Commonwealth Games in Perth (Australia). At that time, running was not a year-round sport. After three months, everything was over. (The first IAAF World Cross-country Championships came in 1973, and Kenya didn't participate until 1981.)

When asked how much he trained in the early sixties, Keino doesn't need time to think. "Training was not all that serious," he says with a mischievous smile on his face. "You woke up in the morning, did your warm-up and some exercises. Later in the day, you would go for a little speed-work. When you went for intervals, maybe once or twice a week when the season approached, you did three or four laps – that's it. And not a lot of mileage. When you work for the police, it is always the same: your duties come first. Running or anything else comes later, maybe at 5 o'clock in the evening. As a policeman, I had to go to different places in the country, places where you could not even run at all. When you came to Nairobi that's when you had training or when you went back to the police college at Kiganjo."

Starting in 1965, Kip Keino was put in charge of physical education at Kiganjo. He was sent to a military school for his training. This also included self-defense. They did different sports, like marching and swimming. He had to teach life-saving and even mountain-rescue, and he coached the football team, too. He became an instructor and an athlete at the same time and had to combine the two things.

Kip Keino with some of his medals

In 1969, he went to England for six months and learned about coaching. "But it was still the same: duty first. You had to wake up your students at 6 for physical education. After breakfast again classes and instructions until 12.30 or 1 o'clock. And then you report again at 2. After 5 that is when you had time for your own training. What we did was basic. Sometimes we had to go for a parade twice a day. And then in the evening you were too tired for any kind of training."

"We could not plan our training for two weeks in advance because you didn't know when you were on duty, sometimes the whole day, sometimes the whole night. We decided more or less from one day to another. First, a retired British military officer was in charge of the training, later it was me. From time to time, we would have some people coming from outside, especially Americans, to give us coaching courses."

Keino wants to make it clear: "Only when we prepared for Commonwealth or Olympic Games did we have enough time for training. Then we were together for one month. But even then we didn't do a lot of mileage. I am telling you, I never reached 60 miles (96 kilometers) a week in my whole life. In the camp, we trained three times a day but not a lot. You warm-up for maybe 5 kilometers, then you run for 2 kilometers and then you do some exercises. Later, you go for your main program. We were doing quality work not mileage. If I did 200s, I did maybe four or six. But jogging in-between was very short. The same with 400 meter intervals: maybe four or six very fast with a very short recovery time. Hill-works also with short repetitions, 150 or 200 meters ten times – that's it. The ones who were putting a lot of mileage didn't last long."

And then the man who was born January 17, 1940, says with a big smile, "It was not training, it was mainly talent. I had a lot of talent – and my running style was beautiful and very smooth. Sometimes I wonder what I could achieve if I were an athlete these days or at least if I would have had more time for training."

In the 1960s and early '70s, there was no money in athletics. Even when you broke a World Record or when the stadium was packed because everybody wanted to see the great duels between Keino and his Australian opponent, Ron Clarke – nothing. The only ones who benefited were the meet promoters. Track and field was a "pure amateur sport." Running was leisure. When Keino was invited to a track meet in London, the organizer would offer the air ticket and a daily allowance of $ 1 US – in later years, it was $ 3 US. At the Olympics, it was $ 3 US a day. At the end of the '60s, there was an IAAF rule stating that athletes were not allowed to stay out of the country for more than a few weeks, otherwise they faced a ban.

Kip himself, later became a professional, like fellow Kenyan Ben Jipcho. He won $ 16,700 US during his first year in professional competitions. After that, he started with his own businesses. He was Kenya's national head coach for a few years. At the 1996 Olympics, he was the Chef de Mission. Since 1999, Kip Keino has been the chairman of the National Olympic Committee of Kenya (NOCK) and he is also a member of the IOC. He is not only the father of Kenyan athletics, he is a legend. He was decorated with a Laureus Award "Sport for Good" and he received many distinctions all over the world, even an honorary doctorate for his humanitarian work – he started an orphanage with his wife, Phyllis, back in the 1980s. An exceptional sportsman he was, an exceptional man he is.

KEINO'S PALMARES

MEDALS

Olympic Games:
  1968 in Mexico, gold at 1,500m, silver at 5,000m
  1972 in Munich, gold at 3,000m steeple, silver at 1,500m
Commonwealth Games:
  1966 in Kingston, gold at 1 Mile and 5,000m
  1970 in Edinburgh, gold at 1,500m, bronze at 5,000m
All Africa Games:
  1965 in Brazzaville, gold at 1,500m and 5,000m
  1973 in Lagos silver, at 1,500m

PERSONAL BEST

400m:	45.8
800m:	1:46.4
1,500m:	3:34.9
1 Mile:	3:53.1
3,000m:	7:39.6 (1965, WR)
5,000m:	13:24.2 (1965, WR
10,000m:	28:06.4
3,000 m Steeple:	8:23.6

TRAINING PROGRAM FOR CROSS-COUNTRY

In 1984, Walter Abmayr, who was the national head coach of the Kenyan Amateur Athletics Association, and his assistant, Michael "Mike" Kosgei, introduced a training program for the cross-country season. The program was still used by Kosgei ten years later as a basis.

The program came with the following guidance:

1. Train regularly without interference.

2. Wear sufficient clothes. Don't use too warm clothes to prevent your body from overheating, vest and shorts are enough for the Kenyan climate in the early part of the year.

3. Gymnastic exercises and stretching are most important before and after a run.

4. Training areas: train in parks, forests and on murrum roads. Avoid tarmac. Hard surfaces provoke injuries.

5. Training is a constant and continuous process. It is not advisable to rest completely before and after a race, but you should go for an easy run, as stipulated in the training program.

6. Care about your well-being. Once you feel very tired and/or overworked in training, don't force yourself too much, instead think about a day off and recover. Mind proper nutrition.

7. Make sure you are physically and mentally prepared before entering in a race. You need to train six weeks before you are ready for a competition.

8. Note: This program is meant for the upper-class distance runners (national level). If it is used by juniors, it has to be slightly modified by cutting 15-20% (duration and intensity). The program is a guideline for athletes and coaches, it cannot refer to individual requirements, such as experience (years of training) and the actual physical conditions (shape/health) of the athlete.

SPEED TABLE FOR ENDURANCE RUNNING

This speed table is recommended for altitude (1,700m and more above sea level). It is important to vary the speed during the different training periods.

Speed D (slow speed)	at a pace of approx.	5'00" per kilometer (men)
		5'25" per kilometer (women)
Speed C (medium speed)	at a pace of approx.	4'30" per kilometer (men)
		4'50" per kilometer (women)
Speed B (higher speed)	at a pace of approx.	4'00" per kilometer (men)
		4'30" per kilometer (women)
Speed A (competitive speed)	at a pace of approx.	3'30" per kilometer (men)
		3'50" per kilometer (women)

Note: Individual differences of approx. 10-15" per km are possible (same level of load)

PHASE/VOLUME	MONDAY	TUESDAY	WEDNESDAY
PREPARATION from 1-30 Nov. (95-105km a week)	M: 14-15km at 70-75' (speed D)	M: -	M: 9-10km fartlek, hilly (sp. D) + 20' gymn.
	A: 4-5km easy, 20' gymn. + strength	A: 10km at 45' (sp. C) + 20' strength	A: -
PREPARATION from 1 Dec.-23 Feb. (120-140km a week)	M: 15-17km at 75-85' (sp. D), + 20' gymn.	M: 10km fartlek, hilly (medium eff.) + 20' strength	M: 18-20km easy (regeneration), + 15' stretch
	A: 5-6km (sp. B), 10x 200m hill + strength	A: 10km at 50' (sp. D)	A: 5km easy, 20' gymn. + strength (with implem.)
PRE-SEASON from 24 Feb.-9 Mar. (140-150km a week)	M: 17-18km at approx. 80' + 20' gymn.	M: 10km fartlek (high effort) + 15' stretch	M: 20km easy (regeneration) + 15' flexibility
	A: 6km (sp. B), 15x 200m hill +20' easy strength	A: 15km at 60' (sp. B)	A: 8km easy + intensive strength
SEASON from 11-17 March (160-170km a week)	M: 18-20km at 75' (sp. B) + 10' gymn.	M: 12km fartlek (high effort) + 10' stretch	M: 25km easy (regeneration) + 15' strength
	A: 10km easy + strength	A: 10km easy, 10' gymn. + 20x 150m hill	A: -
SEASON from 18-24 March (100-110km a week)	M: 14-15km at 60' (sp. B) + 15' stretch	M: 12km fartlek (high effort) + 20' flexibility	M: 15km easy at the WC course
	A: 5km easy, 20' gymn. + 20x 100m hill	A: Flight to Lisbon/POR	A: -

sp. = speed

THURSDAY	FRIDAY	SATURDAY	SUNDAY
M: 18km easy (regeneration)	M: 8-10km at 40-50' (sp. D), 10x 100m (60%) coordination	M: -	M: -
A: 4-5km easy, 20' gymn. + strength	A: -	COMPETITION or 12km at 45' (sp. B)	A: 10-12km at 50-55' (sp. D) + 20' gymn.
M: 15km at 65' (sp. C), 15x 100m (65%) coordination	M: 12km at 55' (sp. C) + 20' gymn.	M: -	M: -
A: 10km fartlek very easy + 15' stretch	A: -	COMPETITION or 13km at 45' (sp. B)	A: 10-12km at 50-55' (sp. D) + 20' flexibility
M: 15km at 60' (sp. B), 20x 100m (70%) coordination	M: 15km at 65' (sp. C) + 20' gymn.	COMPETITION or 13km at 40' (sp. A)	M: -
A: 12km fartlek easy	A: -	A: -	A: 10-12km at 50-55' (sp. D) + 20' flexibility
M: 18km at 70' (sp. B), 20x 100m (75%) coordination	M. 15k at 65' (sp. C) + 20' gymn.	M: -	M: -
A: 12km fartlek (medium effort) + 20' gymn.	A: 12km at 37' (sp. A)	A: 20km at 75-80' (sp. B)	A: 10-12km at 50-55' (sp. D) + strength
M: 15km at 58-60', (sp. B), 10x 100m (85%) coordination	M: 10km at 45' (sp. C) + 15' gymn.	M: 5-8km easy jogging + 10' stretch	IAAF WORLD CROSS
A: 10km fartlek (medium effort)	A: 5-8km easy jogging + 20' strength	A: -	

REMARKS

STRENGTH (Body Conditioning and Circuit Training):

Before the season without implements, e.g., skipping, press-up clap, frog jumps, pocket-knife, stretch-hock-jump, arm-stretch-swing

During the season with implements, e.g., hurdle step-over, different jumps, different throws with medicine ball

STRETCHING: Specific exercises according to the individual deficits

GYMNASTICS: Different exercises, especially for improving the agility

YOBES ONDIEKI'S RECIPE FOR SUCCESS: THE VOLUME

On July 10, 1993, in Oslo, Yobes Ondieki became the first man to run 10,000m under 27 minutes, taking nearly 10 seconds off the five-day-old record set by compatriot Richard Chelimo. Ondieki's time was 26:58.38. Two years earlier, he had won the 5,000m at the World Championships in Tokyo by running away from the whole field on the second lap. The business administration graduate from Iowa State shone in the limelight in 1989 when he became the first man in 10 years to beat Said Aouita at 5,000m.

Ondieki is convinced that the main reason for his big improvement from 1988 to 1989 – from 13:17min to 13:04min in the 5,000m – came because he trained on a regular basis with Peter Koech, the steeplechase Olympic silver medalist of 1988, for 1hr 30 min or even 2 hour-long runs in the early part of the year. "We were together in Albuquerque, and I remember very well, the first time I did a long run with Peter, I was nearly crying," Ondieki recalls. From 1990 onwards when he was based in Flagstaff (Arizona) with his wife, Lisa Martin, he started to train alone, even without a coach, but he carried on with the long runs. Asked about his recipe for success, Ondieki's answer is clear: "The daily volume was high, already as a 5,000 meter runner. I believe when you do a lot of mileage in the first months of the year, sometimes divided in three parts a day, this volume will carry you for the rest of the season. That's why in 1993, for example, I could run three 5,000s within seven days, all under 13:20min. Before I did this volume, sometimes more than 190 kilometers a week, I was a very weak runner." He continues, "Another thing: I was used to running the track sessions alone. I think that is where I got my trademark of front-running."

He was looking forward to winning a medal, maybe even gold, at the Olympics 1992 in Barcelona but things didn't go as expected. He finished fifth. After that, he started focusing on the 10,000m. He increased the volume a little bit, more long runs for improving endurance. Already in the early weeks of 1993, the arrangements were made that he would go for the World Record in Oslo. Ondieki's target was a time of 27:05 minutes. But he wanted to pass at the 5,000m mark in 13:25, "a crazy pace," according to many observers. Ondieki says, "My mind was already set. If I do 13:25 and the second part I ran 13:40, I would still have the record. That was my calculation. In the first 2,000m I felt bad. I think I was not fresh enough after the hard training in Switzerland. As the race progressed, the feeling was better. But after 5,000 meters, I got lost. I could not calculate the pace, I could not count anymore. I only saw Jos Hermens' thumb up. Even if he was not my manager, he helped me a lot. And then it was not until the last lap when I saw something like 25:58." From January until May, Yobes Ondieki trained in Flagstaff. Then he went for some track races to Europe before he did the final preparation in St. Moritz, Switzerland. Here are extracts from his training dairy of 1993.

On the way to his World Record in Oslo

Training at Flagstaff, Arizona/USA, at an altitude of 1,600m above sea level. (You can even run at 2,400 meters.)

Feb. 1	63' (slippery) / 62' (chilly)
Feb. 2	10' warm-up + 5x 800m at 2'09''-2'10'', rec. 2'30'', 5x 400m at 62''-63'', rec. 1', 5' rec. in-between, 15' warm-down / 3km warm-up + 10x uphill
Feb. 3	16km at 62'
Feb. 4	15' warm-up + 1,500m at 4'10'', 15' warm-down / 16km at 58' (chilly, coughed)
Feb. 5	63' for 15km (sore stomach) / 15km at 59'
Feb. 6	1h56' for 31km
Feb. 7	63' for 15km / 10' warm-up + 10x 200m at 32'', rec. 30'', set x2, 5' rec. in between, 10' warm-down
Feb. 8	1h27' for 19km / 30' tempo
Feb. 9	12' warm-up + 2x 100m, 10x 400m at 65'', rec. 1', 10' warm-down / 44' easy
Feb. 10	57' easy / 10' warm-up + 10x 100m, 10' warm-down
Feb. 11	15' warm-up + 4x 800m at 2'12''-2'16'', rec. 2'30'', 10' warm-down
Feb. 12	1h moderate / 10' jog, stretch, 15' jog
Feb. 13	1h30' easy
Feb. 14	2h easy / 12' jog, stretch
Feb. 15	20' moderate + 15x 200m at 34'', rec. 30'', 15' warm-down
Feb. 16	20' easy, 20' easy (sore knee), weights
Feb. 17	53' easy, 10' warm-up + 8x 400m at 63'', rec. 1', 10' warm-down

Feb. 18	12km at 44' = 5'58'' per mile, 12km easy
Feb. 19	12km at 44' (rain the whole day)
Feb. 20	Nothing (weak)
Feb. 21	1h uphill, 1h downhill at Sedona
Feb. 22	12km (flat last 5k) / 10' warm-up + 8x 400m at 64'', rec. 1', 10' warm-down
Feb. 23	12km / 40' easy
Feb. 24	56' easy
Feb. 25	46' easy / travel
Feb. 26	20' jog, 5x 80m strides
Feb. 27	20' warm-up, **15km at 43:13min, race at Tampa, Florida,** warm-down
Feb. 28	Nothing, travel

JUNE 1993

June 1	10km easy / 11km easy / 10km easy / travel
June 2	Nothing / travel
June 3	42' jog at Seville
June 4	36' jog (no sleep) / 25' jog, 5x 100m
June 5	30' easy / 23' jog, **5,000m race in Seville at 13:17.68,** 10' warm-down
June 6	Travel / 40' easy (sore)
June 7	3km warm-up, 1.5km hard + 10x 200m at 27.83'', rec. 30'', 1.5km warm-down / 35' jog
June 8	Nothing (cold, felt bad)
June 9	30' easy / 20' warm-up, **5,000m race in Rome at 13:16.46** (felt bad), 10' warm-down
June 10	30' jog, 4x 100m strides / travel

June 11	20' easy, stretch / 20' warm-up, **5,000m race in Paris at 13:18.41,** 10' warm-down
June 12	Travel Paris-Nairobi
June 13	Travel Nairobi-Eldoret
June 14	Travel Eldoret-Nairobi
June 15	Travel Nairobi-Zurich-St. Moritz

THE LAST THREE WEEKS BEFORE THE WORLD RECORD

Training at St. Moritz, Switzerland, altitude 1,800m above sea level. (You can run in higher areas, too.)

(June 15, arrival from Nairobi via Zurich)

June 16	38' uphill and downhill / 30' jog
June 17	30' jog / 30' jog
June 18	34' around the lake, 5x 100m strides / 4km jog + 5x 400 m at 60.04'', rec. 1', warm-down
June 19	15' warm-up + 10x 400m at 62.80'', rec. 1', 10' warm-down / weights / 30' moderate
June 20	4.3km / 15' warm-up + 3x 1,000m at 2'40.41'', rec. 2', 2x 800m at 2'06.69'', rec. 2', 3x 400m at 59.57'', rec. 1', 5' rec. in between, warm-down / 63' easy jog
June 21	4.3km jog / 63' easy uphill and downhill / 43' uphill and downhill, 5 x 100m
June 22	Nothing (sick, slept the whole day)
June 23	4.3km around the lake / 28' uphill and downhill/ 56' easy uphill and downhill

June 24	4.3km around the lake / 15' warm-up + 20x 200m at 30.59'', rec. 30'', 10x 200m at 29.92'', rec. 30'', 5' rec. in between, 10' warm-down / 48' easy
June 25	8.6km easy / 42' in forest / 15' warm-up + 2x 100m, 2x 2,000m at 5'30.50'', rec. 2', 2x 1,000m at 2'39.54'', rec. 2', 2 x 400m at 59.10'', rec. 1', 5' rec. in between (windy), 15' warm-down
June 26	Nothing
June 27	4.3km easy jog / 4.3km jog, 10' warm-up + 25x 400m at 65.29'', rec. 45''-50'' (felt good), 10' warm-down
June 28	8.6km at 38'-39' / 58' easy uphill and downhill (tired) / 41' easy, 5x 100m
June 29	8.6km moderate / 8.6km easy (tired) / 1.5km jog (rainy)
June 30	10' warm-up + 6x 1,600m at 4'28.40'', rec. 2', 10' warm-down / 8.6km easy

JULY	
July 1	8.6km (chilly) / 1h15' moderate / 4.3km (wet), 5x 100m strides
July 2	8.6km easy / 10' warm-up + 30x 400m at 65.27'', rec. 45''-50'', 10' warm-down
July 3	57' easy / massage / 8.6km easy
July 4	8.6km easy / 10' warm-up + 7x 1,000m at 2'46.13'', rec. 2' (tired), 10' warm-down
July 5	12km easy (legs tired), 1.5km warm-down / 8.6km easy (windy)
July 6	15' warm-up + 10x 400m at 65.96'', rec. 1', 15' warm-down (no push) / 9km very easy / massage

July 7	13km easy (sunny) / 20' jog + 4x 100m, 5x 200m at 32'', rec. 1', warm-down
July 8	8.6km around the lake, stretch, 4 x 100m
July 9	10' jog / travel to Oslo (no sleep, a bit tired)
July 10	20' jog / 20' warm-up, **10,000m in 26:58.38 (WORLD RECORD)**, felt good as race progressed, first 2,000m tired. Splits: 2:41.12/ 5:20.76 (2:39.64)/ 8:02.60 (2:41.84)/ 10:46.42 (2:43.82)/ 13:28.05 (2:41.63)/ 16:10.85 (2:42.80)/ 18:53.55 (2:42.70)/ 21:35.22 (2:41.67)/ 24:20.22 (2:45.00)/ 26:58.38 (2:38.16)
July 11	Travel back to Switzerland (St. Moritz)
July 12	12km easy (tired)
July 13	4km jog
July 14	8km jog + 4x 100m, 8x 400m at 61.30'', rec. 1', warm-down
July 15	13km around the lake / 9km around the lake, 4x 100m
July 16	12km easy
July 17	8km easy (tired) / 15' warm-up + 200m at 28.39'', rec. 1', 400m at 59.19'', rec. 1', 600m at 1'30.28'', rec. 1'30'', 800m at 2'04'', rec. 2', 1,000m at 2'37'', rec. 1'30'', 400m at 60.25'', rec. 1', 400m at 57.82'' (flat), 15' warm-down
July 18	12km around the lake (sunny) / 10' warm-up + 4x 100m, 4x 400m at 56.97'', rec. 1', 10' warm-down

4.3KM = AROUND THE LAKE
8.6KM = TWICE AROUND THE LAKE

REMARKS:

The miles were converted into kilometers

When there are 3 sessions a day, the first one is at 6 a.m., the second one between 10 and 11 and the third one around 4 p.m.

DANIEL KOMEN: TALENT AS A GIFT FROM GOD

He was one of the clearest talents the world of distance running has ever seen. Daniel Komen started his winning streak at the Kenyan Secondary Schools Championships, and as an 18-year-old boy, he returned from the World Junior Championships with two gold medals, in the 5,000 and the 10,000 meters. One year later, he broke the World Junior Records at 1,500m and 5,000m, but he missed out the 1996 Olympics when he was relegated to the fourth position at the Kenyan trials. However, he became the 5,000m World Champion in 1997, and he broke various World Records within three years: 3,000m in 1996, 5,000m in 1997, World Best 2 miles in 1996 and 1997, World Indoor Record 3,000m in 1998 and 5,000m in 1998.

In August 1996, he missed the World Records by the narrowest of margins: 3,000m by 0.05 seconds at Monaco, 5,000m by 0.70 seconds at Zürich, 3,000m by 0.76 seconds at Brussels; then on September 1 came his superb 3,000m at Rieti, in which he took 4.44 seconds off Noureddine Morceli's record, running under 60 seconds for each 400m. This mark of 7:20.67 survived all attempts that came from others, such as Hicham El Guerrouj, Haile Gebrselassie and Kenenisa Bekele. In 1997 he was the first man to run a sub-8 minute two miles at Hechtel, 43 years after Roger Bannister had broken the 4-minute-barrier for the mile. The same year, he lopped 2.12 seconds off Haile Gebrselassie's 9-day-old 5,000m World Record at Brussels. It was the same evening when the Ethiopian lost his 10,000m record to another Kenyan, Paul Tergat.

I still remember when I came to Nyahururu in December 1996. It was the first time we met for an interview. He was dressed casual: blue trousers and a shirt with long sleeves. All of a sudden, he asked me if he should go to his room and change. A few minute later, he came back in a dove-colored double-breasted suit, a white shirt and a black bow tie. "I am sure your readers would like to see a different side of Komen," he said. Fine feathers make fine birds.

Daniel Komen in December 1996

After 1998, Daniel Komen struggled to maintain his form. Looking back, he believes that the two incredibly intensive years, 1996 and 1997, when he used to chase a World Record in almost all his races, took too much energy out of his body.

"In 1996, I had 26 hard races, starting with cross-country and then the track. And 1997 was no different. I think that's why I never got into top gear anymore. My reserves were used up. Runners are not machines where you can go and exchange the engine. But I don't blame anybody. I am very happy with my career," he says.

Daniel Komen has kept most of his training diaries from the '90s. When one sees the training he did at that time, there is nothing spectacular about it. It looks quite conservative, with one exception: he always had a break of two months in September and October – two months without any training. "I was just relaxing," he recalls. "My weight went up from 60 to 65 kilos. The first week of November, that's when I started my training, usually three times a day but very easy, maybe one hour at 6 o'clock, then between 30 and 40 minutes at 10 and another 30 to 40 minutes in the evening. On Sundays, I did a long run of about 1 hour 15 minutes."

"That means a lot of endurance, also hill-work, but all easy, no quality training at all, only to get the body ready and to avoid injuries when you start with the real stuff. April 1 is when the track preparation kicked off. Now more quality came in and also the track workouts. The first few weeks I did the track sessions always in trainings shoes, not in spikes." Usually there were two track workouts a week and one fartlek. What he didn't mention in his diary is all the sprint and strength exercises he did.

Since 1995, Daniel Komen has been coached by Jimmy Beauttah who worked for the British agent Kim McDonald and had a very strong group of athletes at Nyahururu at the time. (See the chapter about Beauttah earlier in this book). Komen used to train with Moses Kiptanui, Paul Bitok, Laban Rotich and Sammy Kipketer. There were more than 20 athletes and everybody wanted to prove that he was ready for a race in Europe. Paul Bitok, two-time Olympic silver medalist at 5,000m, once said, "You know, competitions are easy for us. What is hard is the training."

Daniel Komen ran his first 10,000m race when he was nine. He always liked running. For him, it was a kind of a game. He used to run to school and home three or four times a day about 4 kilometers and during game time he did his serious training of 50 minutes to one hour. He used to wait until the last moment and then run to school as fast as he possibly could to avoid the teacher's punishment. When he saw older boys running, he tried to follow them.

Looking back, Komen says: "My success in athletics is due to Jimmy Beauttah and Kim McDonald and also because I was a very responsible person. When the training was at 6 in the morning, I was ready exactly at 6. I was never late." He then adds, "God has given me the talent. He made me to run very fast and make a lot of money. That's why I try to help people who in their life are not as fortunate as me."

Twice already he went with a car full of clothes and nutrition to the north of the country where the poorest of the poor are living, and where it sometimes doesn't rain for six months. Daniel Komen, one of the most brilliant runners of all time, is also a wonderful human being.

KOMEN'S WORLD RECORDS

3,000m:	7:20.67* (96)
5,000m:	12:39.74 (97)
2 Miles:	8:03.54 (96), 7:58.61* (97)
3,000m Indoor:	7:24.90 (98)
5,000m Indoor:	12:51.48 (98)
1,500m Junior:	3:34.63 (95)
5,000m Junior:	12:56.15 (96)

* Still World Record in spring 2006

JUNE 1997

June 1	30' warm-up + 16x 200m at 26''-28'', rec. 30'' / 40' easy
June 2	45'
June 3	30' warm-up + 8x 200m at 27''-28'', rec. 30'' / 40' easy
June 4	47'
June 5	**Golden Gala Rome:** 30' warm-up, **5,000m 12:48.98 (1.)***
June 6	40' / travel to Russia
June 7	40'
June 8	**Moscow:** 20' warm-up, **3,000m 7:37 (1.)**, heavy rain
June 9	30' / travel
June 10	**Bratislava:** 30' warm-up, **1,500m 3:31.29 (1.)**
June 11	30' / travel to London
June 12	47'
June 13	travel to Kenya
June 14	-
June 15	-
June 16	1h

* 1st position in the race

June 17	1h
June 18	30' warm-up + 4x 500m, 5x 300m, 5x200m (3,000m speed) / 40'
June 19	1h4' / 20' + 30' hill-work / 30'
June 20	47' / 20' warm-up + 2x 500m at 1'17''/1'18'', 5x 300m at 42''/41''/40''/42''/40'', 5x 200m at 27''/26''/26''/27''/27'', rec. 1'30'' / 40'
June 21	59'
June 22	49' / 20' warm-up + 5x 400m at 60''/60''/60''/59''/58'', 5x 200m at 27''/28''/28''/27''/26'', rec. 1'/ 40'
June 23	1h
June 24	49'
June 25	40'
June 26	30'
June 27	30' warm-up, **Kenyan Trials Nairobi**, heat (13:52)
June 28	30' warm-up, **Kenyan Trials Nairobi**, final (1. 13:23)
June 29	44'
June 30	44' / travel to London

JULY 1997

July 1	44' / 30' warm-up + 8x 400m at 60''/60''/58.5''/58''/57''/58''/59''/57'', rec. 1' / 40'
July 2	40'
July 3	30' / travel to Oslo
July 4	**Oslo:** 30' warm-up, **3,000m 7:30.49 (1.)**
July 5	27' / travel to Stockholm
July 6	30'

July 7	**Stockholm:** 30' warm-up, **5,000m 13:01.52 (4.)** (Malaria)
July 8	In the hospital
July 9	In the hospital
July 10	30' / travel to London
July 11	45'
July 12	40'
July 13	30' warm-up + 4x 400m x3 (1st set at 59''/58''/59''/58'', 2nd set at 58''/57''/58''/59'', 3rd set at 55''/57''/56''/55'', rec. 1'), 3' rec. in-between / 40'
July 14	40'
July 15	42'
July 16	30' warm-up + 2x 400m at 55'', rec. 1', 2x 800m at 1'59''/1'58'', rec. 1'30'', 2x 600m at 1'27''/1'28'', rec. 1', 3' rec. in between
July 17	42' / travel to Brussels and Hechtel
July 18	30'
July 19	**Hechtel:** 30' warm-up, **2 Miles 7:58.61 WORLD RECORD**, 400m splits: 58.6, 2:00.4, 2:58.9, 3:58.4 (3:59.8 mile), 4:58.2, 5:56.7, 6:57.5, 7:27.3
July 20	31' / travel to London
July 21	45'
July 22	30' warm-up + 3x 600m at 1'25''/1'27''/1'30'', rec. 1'30'', 3x 600m at 1'27''/1'27''/1'28'', rec. 1'30'', 3x 600m at 1'25''/1'25''/1'27'', rec. 1'30'', 3' rec. in between / 40'
July 23	1h
July 24	45'

July 25	30' warm-up + 200m at 25'', 400m at 54'', 600m at 1'25'', 800m at 1'54'', 600m at 1'25'', 400m at 54'', rec. 2' / 40'
July 26	45'
July 27	30' warm-up + 1,600m at 3'54'', 1,200m at 2'54'', 800m at 1'54'', rec. 3' / 40'
July 28	1h
July 29	30' warm-up + 4x 400m x3 (1st set at 56''/58''/59''/58'', 2nd set at 54''/56''/58''/59'', 3rd set at 60''/58''/59''/60'', rec. 1'), 3' rec. in between / 40'
July 30	42'
July 31	42'

AUGUST 1997

Aug. 1	Travel to Athens
Aug. 2	30'
Aug. 3	30' warm-up + 4x 400m x2 (1st set at 60''/58''/59''/59'', 2nd set at 54''/56''/ 60''/58'', rec. 1'), 3' rec. in-between / 40'
Aug. 4	40'
Aug. 5	40'
Aug. 6	40'
Aug. 7	**Athens World Championships:** 30' warm-up, **5,000m**, heat
Aug. 8	30'
Aug. 9	30'
Aug. 10	**Athens World Championships:** 30' warm-up, **5,000m final: 1. 13:07.38**

Aug. 11	30' / travel to Zurich
Aug. 12	30'
Aug. 13	**Zürich:** 30' warm-up, **5,000m 12:44.90** (2., KNR, 1. Gebrselassie, 12:41.86, WR)
Aug. 14	30' / travel to London
Aug. 15	30'
Aug. 16	30'
Aug. 17	-
Aug. 18	1h
Aug. 19	30' warm-up + 3x 400m at 60''/59''/60'', rec. 1', 3x 300m at 40''/40''/40'', rec. 1', 2' rec. in-between
Aug. 20	42' / travel to Brussels
Aug. 21	30'
Aug. 22	**Brussels:** 30' warm-up, **5,000m 12:39.74** **WORLD RECORD**
Aug. 23	30' / travel to Rieti
Aug. 24	40'
Aug. 25	30'
Aug. 26	**Rieti:** 25' warm-up, **1 mile 3:46.38** (1., KNR)
Aug. 27	- / travel to London
Aug. 28	42'
Aug. 29	30' warm-up + 4x 400m at 52''/52''/52''/53'', rec. 3' / 40'
Aug. 30	30'

TEGLA LOROUPE: POWERS OF RECOVERY

Although she stands only 1.54 meters tall, when it comes to her achievements, Tegla Loroupe is one of the greatest long distance runners of all time. She was three-time World Half-Marathon Champion in 1997, 1998 and 1999, and she broke two Marathon World Records in 1998 and 1999. The only thing missing from her brilliant career is an Olympic or World Championship gold medal. Two World Championships bronze medals at 10,000m in 1995 and 1999 are a little bit mediocre for an athlete of her caliber. On the other hand, she has had eleven wins in 24 marathons, including London, Berlin, New York (two times) and Rotterdam (three times).

Tegla Loroupe with neighbors and relatives

Tegla Loroupe had an amazing 22 days in September and October 1999, when she raced on four successive weekends. First, she won a half-marathon in the Dutch town of Zaandam with a time of 69:20 minutes, then she broke the World Marathon Record in Berlin with 2:20:43 hours. Seven days later, she won the World Half-Marathon Championships in

Palermo (68:48min), and the next week she was second at the Great North Run, Britain's biggest and best-known half-marathon (69:35min).

Her coach and manager, Volker Wagner admits that Tegla Loroupe has always been a little bit special. "Tegla needs only a few weeks of basic training to get in shape. And when she has not been training for four weeks, she was still able to come out and run the 10,000 meters in 33 minutes. What made her so different from others was her power of recovery after a race or a track workout. For example, when she did the 1,000m 20 times at 3'15" and the last ones below 3'10" the recovery in-between was not more than 20 or 25 seconds, and at the end of the workout her heartrate came down to 88 beats per minute after only 60 seconds." The German is still full of admiration when he talks about her. "I think this ability is innate. It meant that Tegla could always do a program of high quality, and her mileage was never more than between 180 and 210 kilometers a week."

Volker Wagner is a mathematics and sports teacher who is now in his mid-fifties. He was a middle distance runner himself. "Good middle class" is how he describes his performances as an athlete. At least, he managed to be a pacemaker in a race where Suleiman Nyambui was running. Nyambui, at that time was the best athlete in Tanzania and in 1980 the Olympic silver medalist at 5,000m. Nyambui became Wagner's first athlete he coached and managed. Then the two Shahanga brothers followed. Nowadays, Volker Wagner coaches about 40 athletes. He bought three cottages in a nearby holiday resort and rented two, so that there is space for 20 athletes at the same time. Recently, he took leave from his job as a teacher. The work as a coach and manager became too much. Also, when you get the agent's percentage for the appearance and prize money from people like Tegla

Loroupe, Joyce Chepchumba, Birhane Adere or the new sensation, Japan based Samuel Wanjiru, you don't have to worry about your future.

It was Walter Abmayr who brought Tegla Loroupe to Germany in 1991, but after a short time she joined Volker Wagner's group. Since then, Detmold, the town next to the "Teutoburger Forest," became Tegla's second home. At the beginning, she was the only woman among men and according to African tradition, she had to wash the clothes and cook the meals. In the meantime, the same athletes became her pacemakers in the marathon races, and she is the most respected athlete in the group.

Tegla's German coach Volker Wagner

Tegla Loroupe thinks the world of Volker Wagner, whom she describes as "a very honest person who knows a lot about running and coaching and a lot about human beings. He is at the same time my physiotherapist, father and friend. I was a nobody when I came to Germany at that time and everything that I have achieved is due to him."

When asked about her amazing power of recovery, Tegla Loroupe talks of her formative years. "Sometimes I ask myself, how it was possible to run, for example, three half-marathons and a full marathon within 22 days. I thank God for giving me the talent and the strength. I am sure it has to do with the way I grew up. When I was a child, I lived for some time with my grandmother. The way to school was 10 kilometers at an altitude of 3000 meters above sea level. For buying maize or corn, we had to go to the valley. We had to walk on one day 50 kilometers and we returned back home the following day, laden with several sacks. I think that is where my toughness comes from."

Tegla Loroupe is an idol to many women in her country and a pioneer in the fight for equal rights. She is also engaged in the battle for peace in her home area, which is West Pokot, not far from the Ugandan border.

TEGLA LOROUPE'S TRAINING PROGRAM MARCH/APRIL 1999

On April 18 she tried to break the Marathon World Record in Rotterdam but failed because of the cold weather. She won the marathon in 2:22:48h. Five months later, she took the record in Berlin, running 2:20:43h. The Japanese, Yoko Shibu, became the first woman to break the 2 hours 20 minutes barrier two years later in Berlin (2:19:41h).

MARCH

March 8	1h easy / 1h easy
March 9	45' easy / warm-up + 15x 1,000m at 3'15''-3'20'', rec. 30''
March 10	1h easy / 1h medium
March 11	warm-up + 10x 1.8km with 400m hill
March 12	1h easy / 1h medium

March 13 1h30' medium

March 14 2h (30' easy, 60' fast, 30' easy)

March 15 1h15' (30' easy, 45' fast) / 1h easy

March 16 45' easy / warm-up + 8x 2,000m at 6'40''
up to 6'20'', rec. 30''-45''

March 17 1h45' (easy-medium)

March 18 1h easy / 1h medium

March 19 Travel to Lisbon / 45' easy

March 20 45' easy

March 21 **Half-marathon Lisbon 67:53min (1.)**

March 22 Travel back to Germany / 45' easy

March 23 1h45 easy-medium

March 24 warm-up + 5x 3km at 10'00'', rec. 1' (forest loop)

March 25 1h30' easy-medium / 1h easy

March 26 1h15' medium / 1h easy

March 27 1h30' medium

March 28 2h15' (30' easy, 60' faster, 30' fast, 15' easy)

March 29 1h15' (30' easy, 45' fast) / 1h15' (30' easy, 45' fast)

March 30 warm-up + 4x 6km with 2km hill fast

March 31 1h45' easy-medium

APRIL

April 1 45' easy / warm-up + 20x 400m at 72''-74'', rec. 20''

April 2 1h30' easy

April 3 **10km race Paderborn 31:23min (5km 15:09min!)**

April 4	1h30' easy
April 5	1h15' medium / 1h easy
April 6	warm-up + 20x 1,000m at 3'20''-3'10'', rec. 20''-35''
April 7	2h easy-medium
April 8	1h15' medium / 1h15' medium
April 9	-
April 10	60' easy
April 11	**10km race Brunssem 31:53min**
April 12	1h15' easy
April 13	warm-up + 20x 400m at 72''-74'', rec. 15''-25''
April 14	60' easy
April 15	Travel to Rotterdam
April 16	45' easy + 5 x sprints
April 17	30'-40' easy
April 18	**Rotterdam Marathon 2:22:48h (1.)** (too cold)

REMARKS:

In 2000, Tegla started running twice a week between 2h and 2h30'. Twice or three times a week, she used to do strength exercises, e.g., 5-10 jumps or sprints (60-80m uphill) – always after easy runs. She did most of her training sessions with men.

PAUL TERGAT'S MARATHON TRAINING: MILEAGE AND QUALITY

Paul Tergat has secured his place in history not only with his Marathon World Record in Berlin at the end of September 2003, but also by winning five consecutive World Cross-Country Championships and breaking various World Records on the track and on the road. Indeed, he is the first man who was able to break the 10,000m World Record and the Marathon World Record, after the Finn Kolehmainen in the nineteen twenties. Tergat is considered one of the greatest runners of all time. In recent years, he has made a name also for his humanitarian commitments.

When he quit the track after the Sydney Olympics and started his marathon preparation at the beginning of December 2000, his longest runs were around 22 kilometers. Now he had to increase his weekly long run gradually, first to 25, then to 30 and finally to 38 kilometers or in other words: up to 2 hours 10, 2 hours 20. As a 10,000m runner, he used to do speed works for half an hour, but now it was up to one hour with intervals and fartlek runs. Until the end of February, Tergat did the training from his home at Ngong outside Narobi. Then he moved to Eldoret, where many athletes, such as Moses Tanui, Elijah Lagat, Joshua Chelang'a, Simon Biwott and Japhet Kosgei, trained for their spring marathon in and around Kaptagat forest, with two sessions a day, often 25 kilometers in the morning and another 15 in the afternoon. On Sundays, they did their long run of 30 to 38km. All in all, he covered between 260 and 280 kilometers a week during the two most intensive months. The last month before the London marathon there were a lot of shorter, faster sessions of 12 or 15km, fartlek and track workouts for regaining speed.

Tergat admitted it was the hardest period of training he had ever done. This was the only time he ever prepared at Kaptagat. Later, he had his training base at home. "My body was not used to an altitude of 2,300m above sea-level. The area around Ngong is only 1,700 or 1,800 meters high. The training at Kaptagat was exhausting. Every evening I was very, very tired," he said.

Paul Tergat finished his first marathon 2001 in London in 2:08:14 hours in second position. It took two and half years and four more marathons before he was able to attack the World Record in Berlin. On September 28, 2003, he was ready to give "master class," Tergat had been very disappointed with his race in London back in April 2003 when he was almost forced to drop out because of stomach problems and was eventually relegated to the fourth position in the final sprint. That's why he started his preparations for Berlin as early as June – first with gym sessions for regaining strength and then with a very demanding three-month program. Before Berlin, he changed the training slightly: more long runs. In the previous marathons he had realized that a lot depends on the mental ability after 38km. That is why he increased his long runs from 38 to 40km and once he

Paul Tergat on the way to his World Record in Berlin

covered 45 kilometers in 2 hours 29 minutes on a difficult course with a tough hill. He ran these 45km so that in the marathon, the 42 would seem somehow short.

Tergat decided to do this immensely long run on his own. It was only after the race that he dared to tell coach, Rosa about it. The mileage increased up to almost 300 kilometers a week. The rest is history. With 2:04:55, Paul Tergat became the first Kenyan to break a Marathon World Record.

PAUL TERGAT'S BASIC MARATHON TRAINING

Week 1

Mon.	1h10' / 1 h
Tue.	35km / 1 h
Wed.	1h15' / 1 h
Thu.	1h15'
Fri.	1h10' / 1 h
Sat.	30' warm-up + 20x 1' fast, 1' slow / 1 h
Sun.	1h10' / 30' + 15 diagonals (180-200m)

Week 2

Mon.	1h10' / 1h
Tue.	30km / -
Wed.	1h10' / 1h
Thu.	30' + 8x 1,000m (2'47''), rec. 1'30'' + 5x 400m (60''), rec. 1'50'' / 1h
Fri.	1h10' / 1h
Sat.	1h15' / 30' + 15 diagonals (180-200m)
Sun.	30km

Week 3

Mon.	1h15' / 1h
Tue.	30' + 25x 1' fast, 1' slow / 1h
Wed.	1h20' / 1h
Thu.	1h10' / 1h
Fri.	30km
Sat.	1h10' / 1h
Sun.	1h15' / 1h

Week 4

Mon.	30' warm-up + 10x 1,000m (2'45''), rec. 1'30'' / 1h
Tue.	1h10'' / 1h
Wed.	1h15' / 1h
Thu.	35km
Fri.	1h10' / 1h
Sat.	1h10' / 1h
Sun.	30' warm-up + 20x 1' fast, 1' slow / 1h

Week 5

Mon.	1h10' / 1h
Tue.	1h15' / 1h
Wed.	30km
Thu.	1h10' / 1h
Fri.	1h15' / 1h
Sat.	30' warm-up + 4x 2,000m (5'42''-5'45''), rec. 2' + 2 x 1,000m (2'45''), rec. 1'30'' / 1h
Sun.	1h10' / 1h

Week 6

Mon.	1h10' / 1h
Tue.	travel
Wed.	1h10' / 1h
Thu.	1h / 50'
Fri.	50' / 40'
Sat.	30'
Sun.	**10km Puerto Rico**

Week 7

Mon.	travel
Tue.	1h10' / 1h
Wed.	1h15' / 1h
Thu.	35km
Fri.	1h10' / 1h
Sat.	30' warm-up + 25x 1' fast, 1' slow / 1h
Sun.	1h10' / 1h

Week 8

Mon.	30' warm-up + 3x 3,000m (8'40''-8'45''), rec. 2' + 2 x 1,000m (2'45''), rec. 1'30''
Tue.	1h10' / 1h
Wed.	1h10' / 1h
Thu.	30km
Fri.	1h10' / 1h
Sat.	40' warm-up + 20x 1' fast, 1' slow / 1h
Sun.	1h10' / 1h

Week 9

Mon.	30' warm-up + 12x 1,000m (2'45''), rec. 1'30'' / 1h
Tue.	1h10' / 1h
Wed.	38km
Thu.	1h10' / 1h
Fri.	40' warm-up + 20x 1' fast, 1' slow / 1h
Sat.	1h10' / 1h
Sun.	1h10' / 1h

Week 10

Mon.	30' warm-up + 10x 1,000m (2'45''), rec. 1'30'' / 1h
Tue.	1h10' / 1h
Wed.	1h10' / 1h
Thu.	travel
Fri.	1h / 50'
Sat.	30'
Sun.	**Lisbon Half-Marathon**

Week 11

Mon.	tavel
Tue.	1h10' / 1h
Wed.	35km
Thu.	1h10' / 1h
Fri.	40' warm-up + 25x 1' fast, 1' slow / 1h
Sat.	1h10' / 1h
Sun.	1h10' / 1h

Week 12

Mon.	30' warm-up + 5x 2,000m (5'42''-5'45''), rec. 2' + 2x 1,000m (2'45''), rec. 1'30'' / 1h
Tue.	1h10' / 1h
Wed.	25km
Thu.	1h10' / 1h
Fri.	40' warm-up + 20x 1' fast, 1' slow / 1 h
Sat.	1h10' / 1h
Sun.	30' warm-up + 2x 5,000m (14'10''-14'15''), rec. 2' + 2x 1,000m (2'45''), rec. 1'30'' / 1h

Week 13

Mon.	1h10' / 30' + 15 diagonals (180-200m)
Tue.	travel
Wed.	30' warm-up + 15 diagonals (180-200m) / 40'
Thu.	50' / 40'
Fri.	50' / 40'
Sat.	-
Sun.	**Marathon**

REMARKS:

The morning training session (around 1h10') is always between medium and fast, the afternoon session (usually 1h) is between slow and medium. The long runs (30-38km) are not slow at all. Tergat's home area (Ngong outside Nairobi) is hilly. The intervals (400m, 1,000m, 2,000m and 3,000m repetitions) are run on the track. When he prepared for the World Record in Berlin, he used the same program except he extended his longest run to 45km (2h29' on a hilly course). In preparation for the Olympics in Athens, he did at least one morning run a week over 1h10' uphill.

ISAAC SONGOK: THE LONG RUNS DON'T EXCEED ONE HOUR

Isaac Songok is one of the most gifted athletes in the world of distance running. Twice he was the National Primary School Champion at 5,000m and in 2001 he became the World Youth Champion at 1,500m. Four years later, he was the bronze medalist at the World Cross-Country Championships (4km) and the winner at the Kenyan trials in the 5,000m.

He trains two or three times a day, depending on the program. An interesting fact: In the months leading to the 2005 Helsinki World Championships, there was not even one training run longer than one hour. Nevertheless, in his first serious year at 5,000m, he managed a formidable 12:52.29. His coach is Brother Colm O'Connell who, up to now, was dealing mostly with 800 and 1,500m runners.

Isaac Songok, national Cross-country Champion at 4km in 2005

Final weeks before the World Cross-Country Championships where he won the bronze medal in the 4km race on March 19.

(Saturday, Feb 12: National Cross-country Championships, 1st at 4km)

Feb. 14	50' easy
Feb. 15	45' easy
Feb. 16	50' easy / - / 30' easy
Feb. 17	40' easy / - / Diagonals
Feb. 18	45' easy / 35' easy
Feb. 19	30' easy / Gym
Feb. 20	60' easy
Feb. 21	45' easy / Fartlek 35' / 30' easy
Feb. 22	50' easy / 30' easy / Exercises 30'
Feb. 23	40' medium / Travel / 30' easy
Feb. 24	50' easy / Fartlek 45' / Exercises 30'
Feb. 25	40' easy / - / Diagonals 35'
Feb. 26	45' easy / HW 10x 200m / 40' easy
Feb. 27	60' easy
Feb. 28	50' easy / Fartlek 45' / 30' easy
Mar. 1	40' easy / - / Diagonals 35'
Mar. 2	45' easy / HW 15x 200m / 40' easy
Mar. 3	40' easy / 30' high speed
Mar. 4	35' medium / 30' easy / Exercises 30'

Mar. 5	50' easy / Fartlek 45' / 30' easy
Mar. 6	60' easy
Mar. 7	50' easy / 35' medium
Mar. 8	40' easy / - / Diagonals 35'
Mar. 9	50' easy / Fartlek 45' / 30' easy
Mar. 10	40' easy / - / Exercises 35'
Mar. 11	45' easy / HW 10x 200m / 40' easy
Mar. 12	30' easy / 35' high speed
Mar. 13	60' easy
Mar. 14	50' easy / 35' medium
Mar. 15	45' easy / 30' high speed / Diagonals 30'
Mar. 16	60' easy

HW: Hill-Work (only for the time before they go to the track, see April/May)

DIAGONALS: Approx. 200m accelerating

EXERCISES: Coordination/Strength/Flexibilty

FARTLEK: In this time of the year, e.g., 3' fast $1^{1/2}$' slow

Competitions: Nakuru April 29 (6. 1,500m 3:44.3), Nairobi May 7 (1. 3,000m 7:46.60), Doha May 13 (4. 1,500m 3:41.94), Hengelo May 29 (1. 3,000m 7:30.14)

Apr. 11	30' easy / Fartlek 40' / Exercises 30'
Apr. 12	40' medium / Track
Apr. 13	30' medium / Striding / 30' easy
Apr. 14	40' high speed / - / Diagonals 40'
Apr. 15	40' medium / Track
Apr. 16	40' medium / Gym / 30' easy
Apr. 17	60'
Apr. 18	40' medium / Track
Apr. 19	30' easy / Diagonals 30' / 40' easy
Apr. 20	40' medium / Track
Apr. 21	40' medium / Gym / 30' easy
Apr. 22	30' high speed / Fartlek 40' / 30' easy
Apr. 23	40' medium / Track
Apr. 24	60'
Apr. 25	40' medium / Track / Diagonals 30'
Apr. 26	30' high speed / Striding / 30' easy
Apr. 27	40' medium / Track
Apr. 28	60' easy / 30' easy / Exercises 30'
Apr. 29	45' medium / **Competition**
Apr. 30	40' medium / Gym / 30' easy
May 1	60'
May 2	40' medium / Track

May 3	30' medium / Diagonals 30' / 30' easy
May 4	40' easy / Striding
May 5	40' medium / Track / Exercises 30'
May 6	60' easy
May 7	45' easy / **Competition**
May 8	60'
May 9	40' medium / - / 30' high speed
May 10	50' easy / Track
May 11	Travel to Doha
May 12	45' easy / - / Optional
May 13	40' easy / **Competition**
May 14	60' easy
May 15	Travel back to Kenya

STRIDING: Different striding patterns flat/curve/uphill/downhill, different distances, all in all, up to 40 min.

TRACK: At this time of the year, between two and three times a week. Starting in the first week with long intervals like 800m or 1000m (3 together), then coming down to faster and shorter ones like 600m, 400m, 300m

DIAGONALS: Approx. 200m accelerating

EXERCISES: Coordination/Strength/Flexibility (set of 10)

REMARKS: When there are three sessions a day, the first one is at 6 a.m., the second one at 10 a.m. and the third one at 4 p.m.

SHAHEEN'S KEYWORD: "PROGRESSIVE"

Stephen Cherono became Saif Saaeed Shaheen in 2003 when he adopted the Qatari nationality. Ten days before the World Championships in Paris, he was cleared by the Kenyan authorities to compete for his new country. Athletics Kenya had agreed to a speedy procedure on the condition the Qatari government built a stadium in the Eldoret area. This failed to materialize however, as the Qatari didn't feel bound to the agreement anymore after the National Olympic Committee of Kenya (NOCK) one year later refused the ex-Kenyan's release for the Athens Olympics.

In the meantime, Shaheen brought two World titles and a World Record to the sheikdom in the Persian Gulf, with the help of his coach, Renato Canova. Canova is an Italian who had worked for Gianni Demadonna since 1999. Demadonna was de manager of Stephen's elder brothers, Christopher Koskei and Abraham Cherono. They were also very successful athletes. Christopher was the steeplechase World Champion in 1999 a nd Abraham the World Junior silver medalist in 1998

Shaheen: training in Kenya

and later the bronze medalist at the Commonwealth Games in 2002. In 2003, he participated at the World Championships, running for Kenya against his Qatari brother.

For many years, Canova worked for the Italian "Federazione Italiana di Atletica Leggera" (FIDAL). Initially, he had been responsible for decathlon and pentathlon, then he was the coach for female marathoners and finally for middle distance runners. In 1986, he became the scientific director of the Italian Athletics Association. When he started coaching Stephen Cherono at the age of 20, the Kenyan was already one of the best steeplechasers in the world: World Youth Champion (1999), World Junior Record holder (7:58.66 in 1999) and Commonwealth Champion. He clearly had more talent than his two brothers. As a youth, Stephen always preferred running the 1.500 meters. "I like 1,500m, you know, but there is a major problem: at my home the steeplechase is a family affair. I have to do what is the family tradition," he says.

When Stephen Cherono changed his citizenship, Canova was offered the job as a coach coordinator for the Qatar Association of Athletics Federation on $ 5,000 US a month

Renato Canova with two of his athletes

plus expenses. The man, who says he never had money in his life, now can stay at the best hotels when he comes to Kenya. The advantage if one has a contract with Qatar is the personal coach always gets the same awards as his athletes. For example, a World Championship title is worth $ 125,000 US. For an Olympic gold, they pay a cool $ 250,000 US. Canova gets very animated when he talks about the luxury he found in Qatar's capital Doha: "The airport is better than the one of Abu Dhabi. They have built a palace with 26 floors for the Olympic Committee. Two floors are used by the athletics federation. Everything is very well organized. Three coaches for distance running are from abroad and the technical director is a former Belgian decathlon record holder."

Only once in a blue moon does Canova have to travel to Qatar. His home is still in Italy. He still spends at least six months in Kenya supervising the training of his best athlete, whom he still calls Stephen, and all the other Qatari ex-Kenyans. They still all train and live in their country of birth. Only one thing has changed: they now need a tourist visa.

Canova's training regime has several key points: Uphill sprints are one of them. However, the main characteristics are the many speed variations and progressive speed, even for the track workouts. They always begin slow and end fast. This is where Shaheen, a.k.a. Cherono, gets his ability to change pace in a race, and that is where his impressive final kick comes from. The program, for the first part of the year, involves long runs up to 1h 20'. The father of two who lives in a beautiful house at Eldoret, in the same neighborhood as Daniel Komen and Moses Tanui, makes no secret that quite often he is shortening these runs. "One good hour is enough for me," he says. Another remarkable aspect is that during the preparation period there is no training on Sundays. This only changes when it comes to the track season, and he would lose too many days traveling to competitions.

Dec. 21	1h progressive / 1h with short speed variations
Dec. 22	30' easy + long fartlek (3x 6' + 3x 3'), rec. 2' easy (39') / 50' easy
Dec. 23	1h moderate / 40' + 6x 30'' skipping + 5x 40m bounding
Dec. 24	1h20' moderate / 50' moderate
Dec. 25	40' + 8x 400m climbing, rec. 3'
Dec. 26	-
Dec. 27	1h10' moderate / 40' + 6x 30'' skipping + 6x 50m bounding
Dec. 28	1h moderate + 15x 80m sprint climbing / 50' easy
Dec. 29	Lap of 22.4km at 1h20' / 45' easy
Dec. 30	1h with short speed variations / 50' + 6x 20m bounding (climbing)
Dec. 31	Track: 3x 2,000m at 5'40'', rec. 3' + 4x 1,000m at 2'45'', rec. 2'
Jan. 1	1h20' moderate-progressive
Jan. 2	-
Jan. 3	50' moderate / 30' + 10x 400m climbing, rec. 3'
Jan. 4	1h20' (30' progressive + 30' fartlek 1' fast, 1' slow + 20' moderate)
Jan. 5	1h / 1h
Jan. 6	30' + 10x 800m (400m climbing to the track + 400m on the track with the lap on the track at 64.0''), rec. 45'' / 40' easy
Jan. 7	1h 20' moderate / 40' + 6x 40'' skipping

Jan. 8	30' easy + 10km hard / 40'
Jan. 9	-
Jan. 10	1h10' progressive (last 20' fast) / 40' + 15x 80m sprint climbing
Jan. 11	Track: 3 sets of 3000m at 8'45'' + 400m at 59.0, rec. 2', 4'-5' rec. in-between
Jan. 12	50' / 50'
Jan. 13	Travel to Edinburgh
(Jan. 15: 9.2km Cross-Country at Edinburgh: position 4)	

TRAINING BEFORE THE 2004 "WELTKLASSE" IN ZÜRICH WHERE HE WANTED TO BREAK THE WORLD RECORD (TRAINING AT ST. MORITZ, SWITZERLAND)

July 28	1h
July 29	1h10' progressive / 40' + 10x 60m sprint uphill
July 30	Track: 2,000m, 1,600m, 1,200m, 800m, 400m at 5'15'' (63'' pace), 4'08'' (62''), 3'03'' (61''), 2'00'' (60''), 54'', rec. 4'
July 31	50' / 50'
Aug. 1	50'
Aug. 2	Track: 3x 600m at 1'33'', 1'30'', 1'27'', rec. 2' + 3x 500m at 1'15'', 1'13'', 1'11'', rec. 2' + 3x 400m at 58'', 56.5'', 55'', rec. 1'30'' + 3x 300m at 42'', 41'', 40'', rec. 1'30'' + 3x 200m at 27'', 26'', 25'', rec. 1'; 5' rec. in between / 30' easy
Aug. 3	40' + strides / 40'
Aug. 4	40'
Aug. 5	40'

Aug. 6	**3,000m steeple World Record attempt in Zürich.** In the training program it is written: Fri, 6 – ZÜRICH (WORLD RECORD!!!). With 8:00.60 he missed out on the record by 5.32 seconds because of a bad job of the pacemakers. – Four weeks later he broke the record in Brussels with 7:53.63.

TRACK SEASON 2005

June 30	Track: 10x 800m at 2'04'', rec. 2'30'' / 40' moderate
July 1	1h10' moderate
July 2	Track: 6x 600m with increasing speed: 1'33'' (rec. 1''), 1'31'' (rec. 2'), 1'29'' (rec. 3'), 1'27'' (rec. 4'), 1'25'' (rec. 5'), 1'23''
July 3	1h moderate
July 4	Track: 10x 400m easy at 60'', rec. 1' / travel to Nairobi
July 5	Travel to Rome / 40' jog
July 6	40' jog / jog and stretching
July 7	30' + strides
July 8	**Rome: 3,000m steeple 7:56.34** (1.)
July 9	40' jog / travel
July 10	Travel to Nairobi / 40' moderate
July 11	1h progressive (last 40' fast) / 30' easy + 15x 80m sprint climbing
July 12	Track: 4x 1,000m at 2'32'', rec. 3' + 4x 600m at 1'28'', rec. 3' + 4x 400m at 56'', rec. 2'; 5' rec. in between / 40' moderate
July 13	1h moderate / 40' easy + technique hurdles and water jump / 40' with speed variations
July 14	1h10' progressive (last 30' fast) / 40' easy + technique
July 15	Track: 10x 800m at 2'02'' (first 5) and 2'00'' (second 5), rec. 3'

TRAINING FOR YOUNG ATHLETES

The training camp at Iten (Rift Valley) is at an altitude of 2,400m above sea-level. It is held in December preparing for the cross-country season when the schools are closed. (There is a similar camp in April.)

The camp is run by Brother Colm, Amos Rono and Joseph Ngure and two assistants.

Almost every day, there are three sessions:

> the first one at 6 a.m.,
> the second one at 10 a.m.
> the third one at 4 p.m.

The mileage varies according to the age and the sex of the athlete. Girls are covering fewer kilometers. These upcoming athletes, some from as far as 100km away, are between 15 and 19 years old. In the second week, for the older boys the mileage reaches 140 kilometers.

Joseph Ngure, Brother Colm and Amos Rono

Day 1	2-4km very easy / 15' warm-up, 2km easy / 6km at 30', 10' warm-down
Day 2	4km very easy / 6km at 25'-30', 20' strength exercises / 7.5km easy at 40'-50', 15' stretching
Day 3	4-6km very easy / 20'-25' strength and flexibility circuit, jog in-between / 8km easy at 40-45'
Day 4	6km very easy / 20' stretching, 8km medium / 6km easy at 30', 20' strength and stretching
Day 5	2-4km very easy / 9-12km at 50'-60' / warm-up and strength exercises, 45' easy-medium
Day 6	6km easy, stretching
Day 7	6-8km medium / 15'-20' stretching, 8-9km easy / 10km easy
Day 8	6-8km (optional) / Fartlek 10km, 5' stretching / 8km easy
Day 9	7-8km fast / 12km easy-medium / strength and coordination exercises
Day 10	8km medium / hill-work 10x 150-200m / 8km easy
Day 11	8-9km easy-medium / 8-10km medium / 6km easy
Day 12	8-9km easy-medium / race pace 8km at 25'-27' (boys), 6.3km at 22'-25' (girls)
Day 13	8-9km easy-medium / 6km, strength and coordination exercises
Day 14	8-10km medium / hill-work 12x 200m, 15'-20' easy / 6-7km easy, 20'-30' circuit
Day 15	8-10km medium / Fartlek 10-14km: 2'-3' fast, 1'-2' easy / 7-9km easy
Day 16	8-9km medium / 8-9km fast (90%) / 6km easy, coordination
Day 17	12-14km very easy / Fartlek 10-12km (1km 60%, 1km 20%) / 40'-50'cross-country
Day 18	7-8km easy / 8-10km medium-fast / 30' Diagonals and accelerations

Before the young athletes leave the Iten training camp, they are given a follow-up program that stipulates two training sessions a day, six days a week. Sunday is considered to be a rest day with optional training. In other words: even 15 or 16 year olds are already training twice a day. This way, an 800m runner will cover 60-80km a week, a 5,000m runner 100-120km.

Running at an early age

WEEKLY TRAINING PROGRAM FOR JUNIORS WHILE THEY ARE AT SCHOOL (TRACK SEASON)

Mon.	Road work: 3-4km (girls), 4-5km (boys) / Intervals on the track: 6x 300m with 100m jog recovery, 6x 200m with 200m jog recovery
Tue.	30' continuous run on the track followed by 10' stretching / Hill-work: 10x 100-120m (girls) and x 14x 100-120m (boys) at 80% effort
Wed.	3-4 laps warm-up on the track followed by coordination and technique at a dynamic speed / Intervals on the track: 5x 400m, 5x 300m with 2' recovery
Thu.	Tempo runs: 100m sprints with 3' recovery for 25' / Hill-work: 12x 100m uphill (flat-out speed) with 100m jog downhill
Fri.	Speed dynamic drills: sprinting diagonals and jog the straights for 20'-30' / Circuit training with 6 stations (star jumps, frog jumps, harness running sit-ups, press-ups, weight lifting, skipping) for 2' with 45" recovery at 85%
Sat.	3-5km road work over a profile area plus 10' stretching / Competition or time trial or interval: 4x 600m with 3' recovery, 4x 400m with 2' recovery
Sun.	Rest / Easy jogging for 35'-45' (optional)

REMARKS: This is a training program for the track season. They run on dirt roads and murrum or grass tracks for three interval and two hill-work sessions a week!

Paul Tergat with his medals

PART 4: STATISTICS

KENYA'S MEDAL WINNERS

First medals: two bronze medals by Bartonjo Rotich at 440 yards hurdles (51.7) and Arere Anentia at 6 miles (28:51.2) at the "British Empire & Commonwealth Games" in 1958 at Cardiff.

OLYMPIC GAMES

First participation in 1956 at Melbourne with eight athletes competing in track and field, two in shooting, a female swimmer and a hockey team. None of the runners advanced to the finals. Four years later in Rome, the best position was sixth place by Nyandika Malyoro at 5000m in 13:52.8.

1964 Tokyo

Ten months after Kenya's independence in December 1963 the team traveled with eleven runners to Japan. Wilson Kiprugut won the country's first Olympic medal, a bronze at 800m. Tokyo was the first Olympic experience for the young Kipchoge Keino. He finished fifth at 1500m and 5000m and missed out on the bronze medal at the longer distance by only 0.6 seconds.

800m: 3. Wilson Kiprugut 1:45.9

1968 Mexico

The high altitude of Mexico City – about 2250m above sea-level – favored the long distance runners from the highlands of East Africa. Kenya won seven individual medals and a silver with the relay, too. Naftali Temu became the country's first gold medal winner after his victory at 10,000m on October 13.

800m:	2. Wilson Kiprugut 1:44.5
1,500m:	1. Kipchoge Keino 3:34.9
5,000m:	2. Kipchoge Keino 14:05.2,
	3. Naftali Temu 14:06.4
10,000m:	1. Naftali Temu 29:27.4
3,000m steeple:	1. Amos Biwott 8:51.0,
	2. Benjamin Kogo 8:51.6
4x 400m:	2. Kenya (D. Rudisha, H. Nyamau,
	N. Bon, Ch. Asati) 2:59.6

1972 Munich

After the successful participation in Mexico, many Kenyans got a scholarship from U.S. colleges. Mike Boit was one of those athletes. Kipchoge Keino increased his number of Olympic medals to four, but the biggest surprise came from the 4 x 400m relay. For the first time, three female athletes were on the team, but none of them advanced to the finals.

400m:	3. Julius Sang 44.92
800m:	3. Mike Boit 1:46.0
1,500m:	2. Kipchoge Keino 3:36.8
3,000m Steeple:	1. Kipchoge Keino 8:23.6,
	2. Ben Jipcho 8:24.6
4x 400 m:	1. Kenya (Ch. Asati, H. Nyamau,
	R. Ouko, J. Sang) 2:59.8

1976 Montreal and 1980 Moscow

Kenya boycotted these Games

In 1976, the Kenyan team was already in Montreal, when it was called back together with other African nations. The reason: a rugby team from New Zealand was on a tour through South Africa, the country that was isolated from the international sports scene because of its apartheid policy. The IOC refused to expel New Zealand from the Games. Four years later, Kenya joined the boycott, initiated by the USA after the invasion of the Soviet Union in Afghanistan. The ones to suffer most were Mike Boit, the star at 800m, and long distance runner, Henry Rono.

1984 Los Angeles

The two boycotts had a devastating effect. Kenya had lost contact with the world-leading athletes in most of the disciplines and traveled with a young team to Los Angeles. Nevertheless, Julius Korir made sure that a Kenyan was on the top of the steeplechase for the third time in a row; the young Julius Kariuki finished fourth. Mike Musyoki was awarded with the bronze medal at 10,000m only after the second placed Finn, Martti Vainio, was disqualified because of a positive doping test. Ruth Waithera in eighth position at 400m was the first female Kenyan in an Olympic final.

10,000m: 3. Mike Musyoki 28:06.46
3,000m Steeple: 1. Julius Korir 8:11.80

1988 Seoul

With four victories, their most successful Olympic participation, even if there was one medal more 1968 in Mexico. From the Seoul medal winners, Paul Ereng, Peter Rono, Julius Kariuki and Peter Koech were students in the USA, Douglas Wakiihuri lived in Japan, Kipkemboi Kimeli most of the time in Germany. Only army sergeant, John Ngugi, was a "real" Kenyan.

800m:	1. Paul Ereng 1:43.45
1,500m:	1. Peter Rono 3:35.96
5,000m:	1. John Ngugi 13:11.70
10,000m:	3. Kipkemboi Kimeli 27:35.16
3,000m Steeple:	1. Julius Kariuki 8:05.51,
	2. Peter Koech 8:06.79
Marathon:	2. Douglas Wakiihuri 2:10:47

1992 Barcelona

Kenya was represented in track and field by 33 male and 9 female athletes. The result: 2 gold medals and the first "clean sweep" in Kenya's classic event, the 3,000m steeplechase. Controversy arose in the final of 10,000m when Khalid Skah was being helped by his lapped countryman Boutayeb; first he was disqualified and later reinstalled as the winner.

400m:	3. Samson Kitur 44.24
800m:	1. William Tanui 1:43.66,
	2. Nixon Kiprotich 1:43.70
5,000m:	2. Paul Bitok 13:12.71
10,000m:	2. Richard Chelimo 27:47.72
3,000m Steeple:	1. Matthew Birir 8:08.84,
	2. Patrick Sang 8:09.55,
	3. William Mutwol 8:10.74

1996 Atlanta

The big surprise from the Kenyan point of view happened in the steeplechase final where triple World Champion and World Record holder, Moses Kiptanui, lost to his training partner, Joseph Keter, in the final sprint. Marathon bronze medal winner, Eric Wainaina, lived and trained in Japan, as did Wakiihuri. Pauline Konga, Paul Bitok's wife, was the first Kenyan female athlete to win an Olympic medal.

800m:	3. Fred Onyancha 1:42.79
1,500m:	3. Stephen Kipkorir 3:36.72
5,000m:	2. Paul Bitok 13:08.16

10,000m:	2. Paul Tergat 27:08.17
3,000m Steeple:	1. Joseph Keter 8:07.12,
	2. Moses Kiptanui 8:08.33
Marathon:	3. Eric Wainaina 2:12:44

Women

5000m:	2. Pauline Konga 15:03.49

2000 Sydney

Sensation Noah Ngeny beat the "unbeatable" Moroccan Hicham El Guerrouj in the 1,500m final. At 10,000m, Paul Tergat seemed to be on the way winning his first gold after three silver medals at World Championships and Olympic Games, but at the end he was again caught by Haile Gebrselassie. After 10,000 meters, there were only 0.09 seconds between the two – the closest outcome in the event's history.

1,500m:	1. Noah Ngeny 3:32.07,
	3. Bernard Lagat 3:32.44
10,000m:	2. Paul Tergat 27:18.29
3,000m Steeple:	1. Reuben Kosgei 8:21.43,
	2. Wilson Boit Kipketer 8:21.77
Marathon:	2. Eric Wainaina 2:10:31

Women

Marathon:	3. Joyce Chepchumba 2:24:45

2004 Athen

Ezekiel Kemboi benefited from the absence of the neo-Qatari Saif Saaeed Shaheen, who didn't get clearance from the National Olympic Committee of Kenya. It was Kenya's eighth Olympic gold medal in the steeplechase. Biggest disappointment: Marathon World Record holder Paul Tergat had stomach problems and finished in tenth position.

1,500m:	2. Bernard Lagat 3:34.30
5,000m:	3. Eliud Kipchoge 13:15.10

3,000m Steeple:	1. Ezekiel Kemboi 8:05.81,
	2. Brimin Kipruto 8:06.11,
	3. Paul K. Koech 8:07.18

Women

| 5,000m: | 2. Isabella Ochichi 14:48.19 |
| Marathon: | 2. Catherine Ndereba 2:26:32 |

WORLD CHAMPIONSHIPS

1983 Helsinki

No medals

1987 Rome

Four years after the "zero payday" at Helsinki, Kenya won three medals – and all in gold. Billy Konchellah celebrated the first of his two titles. A negative surprise at 3,000m steeplechase: after the victory at the last Olympics this time not even a medal.

800m:	1. Billy Konchellah 1:43.06
10,000m:	1. Paul Kipkoech 27:38.63
Marathon:	1. Douglas Wakiihuri 2:11:48

1991 Tokyo

The best record in the history of the World Championships with 8 positions in the top three, among them 4 gold medals. The beginning of Moses Kiptanui's reign. First medal for a female Kenyan runner by Susan Sirma.

800m:	1. Billy Konchellah 1:43.99
1500m:	2. Wilfred Kirochi 3:34.84
5000m:	1. Yobes Ondieki 13:14.45
10,000m:	1. Moses Tanui 27:38.74,
	2. Richard Chelimo 27:39.41
3000m Steeple:	1. Moses Kiptanui 8:12.59,
	2. Patrick Sang 8:13.44

Women

| 3000m: | 3. Susan Sirma 8:39.41 |

1993 Stuttgart

Third win in a row at 800m, this time by the surprising Paul Ruto. Again 8 medals, but "only" 3 in gold. Second double by Moses Kiptanui and Patrick Sang in the steeple.

800m:	1. Paul Ruto 1:44.71,
	3. Billy Konchellah 1:44.89
5,000m:	1. Ismael Kirui 13:02.75
10,000m:	2. Moses Tanui 27:46.54,
	3. Richard Chelimo 28:06.02
3000m Steeple:	1. Moses Kiptanui 8:06.36,
	2. Patrick Sang 8:07.53

Women

10,000m:	3. Sally Barsosio 31:19.38

1995 Gothenburg

Ismael Kirui, brother to Richard Chelimo, triumphed for the second time in a row at 5,000m and was awarded with a second Mercedes car, which he is still driving after ten years. Moses Kiptanui won his third World Championship gold.

5,000m:	1. Ismael Kirui 13:16.77,
	3. Shem Kororia 13:17.59
10,000m:	3. Paul Tergat 27:14.70
3,000m Steeple:	1. Moses Kiptanui 8:04.16,
	2. Christopher Koskei 8:09.30

Women

10,000m:	3. Tegla Loroupe 31:17.66

1997 Athens

Six years after Susan Sirma's bronze medal in Tokyo, Sally Barsosio became the first woman from Kenya to win a World Championship title.

5,000m:	1. Daniel Komen 13:07.38,
	3. Tom Nyariki 13:11.09

10,000m:	2. Paul Tergat 27:25.62
3,000m Steeple:	1. Wilson Boit Kipketer 8:05.84,
	2. Moses Kiptanui 8:06.04,
	3. Bernard Barmasai 8:06.04

Women

| 10,000m: | 1. Sally Barsosio 31:32.92 |

1999 Seville

Christopher Koskei, the older brother of Stephen Cherono, a.k.a. Saif Saaeed Shaheen, proved to be Kenya's savior with the only gold. Nevertheless, a disappointing outcome with six medals overall. Tergat won his third medal in a row.

1,500m:	2. Noah Ngeny 3:28.73
5,000m:	2. Benjamin Limo 12:58.72
10,000m:	2. Paul Tergat 27:58.56
3,000m Steeple:	1. Christopher Koskei 8:11.76,
	2. Wilson Boit Kipketer 8:12.09

Women

| **10,000m:** | 3. Tegla Loroupe 30:32.03 |

2001 Edmonton:

At 10,000m, Charles Kamathi ended the dominance of Ethiopia's Haile Gebrselassie who was three-time World Champion at the distance and now finished only third. One year after becoming Olympic Champion, Reuben Kosgei claimed the world title at 3,000m steeplechase. But after that, he had a lot of injury problems. For the first time since 1987, no medal for Kenya's women.

800m:	2. Wilfred Bungei 1:44.55
1,500m:	2. Bernard Lagat 3:31.10
5,000m:	1. Richard Limo 13:00.77,
	3. John Kibowen 13:05.20
10,000m:	1. Charles Kamathi 27:53.25

3,000m Steeple:	1. Reuben Kosgei 8:15.16,
	3. Bernard Barmasai 8:16.59
Marathon:	2. Simon Biwott 2:12:43

2003 Paris

After winning six consecutive finals at 3,000m steeplechase, no gold medal for the Kenyans this time. Cold comfort that Saif Saaeed Shaheen, a Qatari, won, who a few weeks ago was still a Kenyan with the name of Stephen Cherono.

| **5,000m:** | 1. Eliud Kipchoge 12:52.79 |
| **3,000m Steeple:** | 2. Ezekiel Kemboi 8:05.11 |

Women
| **5,000m:** | 3. Edith Masai 14:52.30 |
| **Marathon:** | 1. Catherine Ndereba 2:23:55 |

2005 Helsinki

Thanks to their female athletes who managed to win 2 gold, 2 silver and 2 bronze (the men only 1 gold and 2 silver) for the first time, Ethiopia was a far cry from Kenya, but considering all the places in the finals, there was only one point between the two rivals. Six years after winning a silver medal at Seville, Benjamin Limo surprisingly won the 5000m. With the 20-year-old Moses Mosop, a new long distance hope arose.

800m:	3. William Yiampoy 1:44.55
5,000m:	1. Benjamin Limo 13:22.55
10,000m:	3. Moses Mosop 27:08.96
3,000m Steeple:	2. Ezekiel Kemboi 8:14.95,
	3. Brimin Kipruto 8:15.30

Women
| **3,000m Steeple:** | 3. Jeruto Kiptum 9:26.95 |
| **Marathon:** | 2. Catherine Ndereba 2:22:01 |

Sally Barsosio

KENYAN WORLD RECORD HOLDERS

3,000m

7:39.6	Kipchoge Keino	27.08.65	Hälsingborg
7:32.1	Henry Rono	27.06.78	Oslo
7:28.96	Moses Kiptanui	16.08.92	Cologne
7:20.67	Daniel Komen	01.09.96	Rieti

Record holder in spring 2006:

7:20.67	Daniel Komen (KEN)	01.09.96	Rieti

5,000m

13:24.2	Kipchoge Keino	30.11.65	Auckland
13:08.4	Henry Rono	08.04.78	Berkeley
13:06.20	Henry Rono	13.09.81	Knarvik
12:55.30	Moses Kiptanui	08.06.95	Rome
12:39.74	Daniel Komen	22.08.97	Brussels

Record holder in spring 2006:

12:37.35	Kenenisa Bekele (ETH)	31.05.04	Hengelo

10,000m

27:30.5	Samson Kimobwa	30.07.77	Helsinki
27:22.4	Henry Rono	11.06.78	Vienna
27:07.91	Richard Chelimo	05.07.93	Stockholm
26:58.38	Yobes Ondieki	10.07.93	Oslo
26:52.23	William Sigei	22.07.94	Oslo
26:27.85	Paul Tergat	22.08.97	Brussels

Record holder in spring 2006:

26:17.53	Kenenisa Bekele (ETH)	26.08.05	Brussels

Half-marathon

60:24	Benson Masya	20.09.92	Newcastle
59:47	Moses Tanui	03.04.93	Milan
59:17	Paul Tergat	04.04.98	Milan
59:16	Samuel Wanjiru	11.09.05	Rotterdam

Record holder in spring 2006:

58:55	Haile Gebrselassie (ETH)	15.01.06	Phoenix

Marathon

2:04:55	Paul Tergat	28.09.03	Berlin

Record holder in spring 2006:

2:04:55	Paul Tergat (KEN)	28.09.03	Berlin

3,000m Steeplechase

8:19.8	Benjamin Jipcho	19.06.73	Helsinki
8:14.0	Benjamin Jipcho	27.06.73	Helsinki
8:05.4	Henry Rono	13.05.78	Seattle
8:05.35	Peter Koech	03.07.89	Stockholm
8:02.08	Moses Kiptanui	19.08.92	Zurich
7:59.18	Moses Kiptanui	16.08.95	Zurich
7:59.08	Wilson Boit Kipketer	13.08.97	Zurich
7:55.72	Bernard Barmasai	24.08.97	Cologne

Record holder in spring 2006:

7:53.63	Saif Saaeed Shaheen (QAT, former Stephen Cherono, KEN)	03.09.04	Brussels

There has never been a Kenyan World Record holder at distances shorter than 3,000m. (Wilson Kipketer, 800m 1:41.11min, is Kenyan born, but running for Denmark.)

The only Kenyan women to break a World Record were Tegla Loroupe and Catherine Ndereba in the marathon. In half-marathon, Susan Chepkemei ran 65:44 in Lisbon 2001, the fastest time in the world so far, but the course was 60m downhill. Therefore, the time was not recognized as a World Record.

Marathon women

2:20:47	Tegla Loroupe	19.04.98	Rotterdam
2:20:43	Tegla Loroupe	26.09.99	Berlin
2:18:47	Catherine Ndereba	07.10.01	Chicago

Record holder in spring 2006:

2:15:25	Paula Radcliffe (GBR)	13.04.03	London

KENYA COMPARED WITH ETHIOPIA

POSITIONS IN THE TOP 100

1985

MEN

800m:	KEN 5, ETH 0	(1. USA 15)
1,500m:	KEN 8, ETH 0	(1. USA 11)
5,000m:	KEN 6, ETH 1	(1. USA 24)
10,000m:	KEN 6, ETH 4	(1. USA/SU 16)
3000m Steeple:	KEN 9, ETH 0	(1. USA 17)
Marathon:	KEN 5, ETH 3	(1. JAP 13)

WOMEN

800m:	KEN 0, ETH 0	(1. SU 34)
1,500m:	KEN 0, ETH 0	(1. SU 34)
3,000m:	KEN 0, ETH 0	(1. SU 26)
10,000m:	KEN 0, ETH 0	(1. SU 25)
Marathon:	KEN 0, ETH 0	(1. SU 17)

2005

MEN

800m:	KEN 23 (1.), ETH 0
1,500m:	KEN 24 (1.), ETH 2
5,000m:	KEN 43 (1.), ETH 14
10,000m:	KEN 42 (1.), ETH 10
3,000m Steeple:	KEN 24 (1.), ETH 2
Half-marathon:	KEN 66 (1.), ETH 10
Marathon:	KEN 52 (1.), ETH 9

WOMEN

800m:	KEN 3, ETH 0	(1. RUS 24)
1,500m:	KEN 2, ETH 3	(1. RUS 21)
5,000m:	KEN 17 (1.), ETH 14	
10,000m:	KEN 16, ETH 9	(1. JAP 36)
Half-marathon:	KEN 22, ETH 9	(1. JAP 41)
Marathon:	KEN 16, ETH 11	(1. JAP 19)

MEDALS:

Olympic Games

Kenya: Men: 16 Gold,   20 Silver,   14 Bronze
           Women: 3 Silver,   1 Bronze

Ethiopia: Men: 10 Gold,   3 Silver,   8 Bronze
           Women: 4 Gold,   2 Silver,   4 Bronze

World Championship

Kenya: Men: 20 Gold,   18 Silver,   12 Bronze
           Women: 2 Gold,   1 Silver,   6 Bronze

Ethiopia: Men: 7 Gold,   8 Silver,   5 Bronze
           Women: 6 Gold,   5 Silver,   6 Bronze

Cross-Country World Championships (until 2005)

Kenya: Men: 40 Gold,   22 Silver,   20 Bronze
           Women: 13 Gold,   12 Silver,   11 Bronze
           Junior Men: 29 Gold,   17 Silver,   11 Bronze
           Junior Women: 18 Gold,   15 Silver,   11 Bronze

Ethiopia: Men: 19 Gold,   19 Silver,   17 Bronze
           Women: 21 Gold,   20 Silver,   8 Bronze
           Junior Men: 17 Gold,   26 Silver,   8 Bronze
           Junior Women: 12 Gold,   10 Silver,   7 Bronze

THE BEST AFRICAN PERFORMERS 1965 - 2005

MEN

	800m	1500m	5000m
1965	Kiprugut KEN 1:47.4	Keino KEN 3:37.6	Keino KEN 13:24.2
1975	Boit KEN 1:43.79	Bayi TAN 3:35.0	N'geno KEN 13:26.8
1985	Konchellah KEN 1:43.72	Aouita MOR 3:29.46	Aouita MOR 13:00.40
1995	B. Koech KEN 1:43.45	Morceli ALG 3:27.37	Gebrselassie ETH 12:44.39
2005	Bungei KEN 1:43.70	D.K. Komen KEN 3:29.72	Bekele ETH 12:40.18

WOMEN

	800m	1500m	3000m/5000m*
1975	Chemabwai KEN 2:05.8	Tata KEN 4:19.0	Derouich TUN 9:57.4
1985	Peckham RSA 2:02.24	Peckham RSA 4:10.6	Van Zyl RSA 8:58.73
1995	Motola MOZ 1:55.72	Motola MOZ 4:01.6	Meyer RSA 14:44.05
2005	Jepkosgei KEN 1:57.82	Bati ETH 3:59.60	Defar ETH 14:28.98

10,000 m	Marathon	3000m St
Gammoudi TUN 28:56.2	Bikila ETH 2:22:54	Bel Azzou MOR 8:45.6
N'geno KEN 28:04.6	Rakabele ETH 2:16:06	Mohamed ETH 8:19.57
Kigen KEN 27:43.9	Robleh DJI 2:08:08	P. Koech KEN 8:19.84
Gebrselassie ETH 26:43.53	Lelei KEN 2:07:02	Kiptanui KEN 7:59.18
Bekele ETH 26:17.53	Gebrselassie ETH 2:06:20	Koech KEN 7:56.37

10,000 m	Marathon	3000m St
+	+	-
Darami MOR 33:46.69	Joubert RSA 2:35:45	-
Tulu ETH 31:08.10	Meyer RSA 2:26:51	-
T. Dibaba ETH 30:15.67	Ndereba KEN 2:22:01	Inzikuru UGA 9:15.04

* At the WC 1995 in Gothenburg the 5000m became the official distance for women at championships

\- 3,000m steeplechase became a championship event in 2005

\+ Before 1980 there were no official records for 10,000m and Marathon women

PHOTO CREDITS

Cover design: Jens Vogelsang, Germany
Cover photo: Jürg Wirz
Back cover photos: Jürg Wirz

All inside photos by Jürg Wirz except:
Beyond the Finish line: p. 16, 50, 53
The Standard: p. 27
Walter Abmayer: p. 30, 84/85
Archiv Abmayer: p. 60, 61, 190/191
Top Distance Runners of the Century: p. 128
Brian J. Myers/WFP United Nations: p. 150